Mexico's Drug War and Criminal Networks

Mexico's Drug War and Criminal Networks examines the effects of technology on three criminal organizations: the Sinaloa cartel, the Zetas, and the Caballeros Templarios.

Using social network analysis, and analyzing the use of web platforms Facebook, Twitter, and YouTube, Nilda M. Garcia provides fresh insights on the organizational network, the central nodes, and the channels through which information flows in these three criminal organizations. In doing so, she demonstrates that some drug cartels in Mexico have adopted the usage of social media into their strategies, often pursuing different tactics in the search for new ways to dominate. She finds that the strategic adaptation of social media platforms has different effects on a criminal organization's ability to survive. When used effectively, coupled with the adoption of decentralized structures, these platforms do increase a criminal organization's survival capacity. Nonetheless, if used haphazardly, they can have the opposite effect.

Drawing on the fields of criminology, social network analysis, international relations, and organizational theory, and featuring a wealth of information about the drug cartels themselves, *Mexico's Drug War and Criminal Networks* will be a great source for all those interested in the presence, behavior, purposes, and strategies of drug cartels in their forays into social media platforms in Mexico and beyond.

Nilda M. Garcia is a Visiting Assistant Professor at the Political Science Department at Texas A & M International University. She teaches courses in international politics, foreign policy, American and State government, political economy of development, and drug trafficking. Her research interests include organized crime, drug trafficking, international relations, and security studies.

Routledge Advances in International Relations and Global Politics

143 **The Duty of Care in International Relations**
Protecting Citizens Beyond the Border
Nina Graegar and Halvard Leira

144 **The Global Politics of Jazz in the Twentieth Century**
Cultural Diplomacy and "American Music"
Yoshiomi Saito

145 **South Africa and the UN Human Rights Council**
The Fate of the Liberal Order
Eduard Jordaan

146 **Economic Sanctions in International Law and Practice**
Edited by Masahiko Asada

147 **Iran in the International System**
Between Great Powers and Great Ideas
Edited by Heinz Gärtner and Mitra Strohmaier

148 **International Relations as Politics Among People**
Hannes Hansen-Magnusson

149 **Mexico's Drug War and Criminal Networks**
The Dark Side of Social Media
Nilda M. Garcia

150 **Transnational Labour Migration, Livelihoods and Agrarian Change in Nepal**
The Remittance Village
Ramesh Sunam

For information about the series: www.routledge.com/Routledge-Advances-in-International-Relations-and-Global-Politics/book-series/IRGP

Mexico's Drug War and Criminal Networks

The Dark Side of Social Media

Nilda M. Garcia

LONDON AND NEW YORK

First published 2020 by Routledge
2 Park Square, Milton Park, Abingdon, Oxon OX14 4RN
605 Third Avenue, New York, NY 10017

Routledge is an imprint of the Taylor & Francis Group, an informa business

First issued in paperback 2021

Copyright © 2020 Taylor & Francis

The right of Nilda M. Garcia to be identified as author of this work has been asserted by her in accordance with sections 77 and 78 of the Copyright, Designs and Patents Act 1988.

All rights reserved. No part of this book may be reprinted or reproduced or utilised in any form or by any electronic, mechanical, or other means, now known or hereafter invented, including photocopying and recording, or in any information storage or retrieval system, without permission in writing from the publishers.

Notice:
Product or corporate names may be trademarks or registered trademarks, and are used only for identification and explanation without intent to infringe.

Publisher's Note

The publisher has gone to great lengths to ensure the quality of this reprint but points out that some imperfections in the original copies may be apparent.

Library of Congress Cataloging-in-Publication Data
A catalog record for this title has been requested

ISBN: 978-0-367-33496-3 (hbk)
ISBN: 978-1-03-217290-3 (pbk)
DOI: 10.4324/9780429320309

Typeset in Sabon
by Wearset Ltd, Boldon, Tyne and Wear

Contents

List of Figures vi
List of Graphs vii
List of Maps viii
List of Tables ix

Introduction 1

1 Narco Mexico 15

2 Social Media: The Continuation of War by Other Means 36

3 The Sinaloa Cartel 52

4 The Zetas Cartel 75

5 The Caballeros Templarios 104

Conclusion 130

Appendix 141
Index 142

Figures

0.1	Survival Capacity of Criminal Organizations and Social Media Usage Model	9
3.1	Sinaloa Cartel's Response to Organizational Shocks 2006–2015	59
3.2	Sinaloa Cartel's Twitter Usage and Organizational Shocks 2006–2015	69
4.1	The Zetas' Response to Organizational Shocks 2006–2015	84
4.2	The Zetas' Facebook Network	87
4.3	The Zetas' Facebook Usage and Organizational Shocks 2006–2015	96
5.1	Caballeros Templarios' Response to Organizational Shocks 2011–2015	112
5.2	Caballeros Templarios' Facebook Network	114
5.3	Caballeros Templarios' YouTube Usage and Major Organizational Shocks 2011–2015	122

Graphs

3.1	Sinaloa Cartel's Reported Clashes 2006–2015	56
3.2	Sinaloa Cartel's Twitter Network	62
3.3	Sinaloa Cartel's Twitter Content Analysis	64
3.4	Sinaloa Cartel's YouTube Content Analysis	66
3.5	Sinaloa Cartel's Twitter Usage and Reported Clashes 2006–2015	70
4.1	The Zetas' Reported Clashes 2006–2015	80
4.2	The Zetas' Facebook Content Analysis	90
4.3	The Zetas' YouTube Content Analysis	92
4.4	The Zetas' Share of Threats	93
4.5	The Zetas' Facebook Usage and Reported Clashes	97
5.1	Caballeros Templarios' Reported Clashes 2011–2015	109
5.2	Caballeros Templarios' Facebook Content Analysis	116
5.3	Caballeros Templarios' YouTube Content Analysis	117
5.4	Caballeros Templarios' Reported Clashes and Facebook Use 2011–2015	123
5.5	Caballeros Templarios' Reported Clashes and YouTube Usage 2011–2015	124

Maps

0.1 Main Areas of Influence of the Major Mexican
    Drug Cartels   5
4.1 Twitter Hashtag Usage per Region   99

Tables

3.1	Sinaloa Cartel Regression, Clashes and Social Media Use	71
4.1	Correlation between the Zetas' Facebook Presence and Reported Clashes	97
4.2	The Zetas Regression, Facebook Use	98
4.3	The Zetas Regression, Twitter Use	98
5.1	Correlation between Caballeros Templarios' YouTube Presence and Reported Clashes	117
5.2	Caballeros Templarios Regression, Facebook Use	125
5.3	Caballeros Templarios Regression, YouTube Use	125
6.1	Summary of Empirical Findings	135

Introduction

There is a dark side to social media. Technology, the internet, and social media platforms have transformed the way we communicate. These communication outlets have made it possible for individuals from around the world to connect almost instantly, and to freely express their opinions or report virtually anything. The web is still a highly unregulated space where users can maintain complete anonymity, and it is nowadays highly accessible to everyone with internet access, including terrorists and criminal organizations (COs).

The rapid increase in the use of social media[1] during the "war on drugs" in Mexico, especially in the first decades of the twenty-first century, has stimulated a growing research agenda. To date, this scholarship has focused primarily on investigating the opportunities social media platforms such as Facebook, Twitter, and YouTube offer to civilians as organizing mechanisms, to fill the informational vacuum left by the tightly self-censored mainstream media outlets, and as a tool for survival. Yet, the use of these platforms has taken a darker, more sinister turn. Research exploring the use of social media platforms in Mexico has not emphasized the fact that these communication outlets provide major opportunities for drug cartels or criminal organizations to engage in public relations strategies, ease their recruitment tactics, send threatening messages to government authorities and civilians, and warn off potential rivals.

The drug war in Mexico is one of the most brutal conflicts in the world with about 332,000 drug-related homicides since 2006 (Calderón, Heinle, Rodríguez Ferreira, & Shirk, 2019). Despite the declared victories from the government, the strategy followed by Felipe Calderón (2006–2012) and by the Peña Nieto administration (2012–2018) to combat the drug cartels was far from successful. We are yet to evaluate the drug policy approach of current president Andrés Manuel López Obrador. Indicators of violence, however, demonstrate that 2019 will close as the most violent year, with the highest homicide rate of the last 25 years. Notwithstanding the efforts of these administrations, domestic security remains difficult to achieve because of the highly volatile, violent, and extremely competitive environment in which some criminal organizations like the Sinaloa cartel or the Zetas have managed to not only survive, but also grow in influence, size, and power more than other criminal organizations during the years of this study. The landscape of drug trafficking in Mexico is constantly changing, giving rise to newer and stronger organizations which have gained momentum. One such is the Cartel Jalisco Nueva Generación (CJNG), considered the main contender to the Sinaloa cartel, and another the Cartel del Noreste (CDN), which originated from the Zetas (now Zetas Old School), becoming its own cartel in 2018.

Since the militarization of the war on drugs in 2006, the media has played an important role in the conflict. Both the government and the drug cartels have for years controlled the flow of information from mainstream media outlets, using it strategically for propaganda purposes. In order to block the criminal organizations from taking advantage of the media exposure, 715 Mexican media channels signed an agreement in 2011 to censor reports about the drug war and to follow particular editorial criteria when informing the public about organized crime–related violence.[2] Following this collective response, the use of social media, by both civilians and cartels, boomed in the country.[3] In some areas affected by the hyper-violence triggered by the drug war, social media has been used by the citizenry as an alternative outlet to get information about shootings or blockades by cartels. At the same time, some drug trafficking organizations also embrace these web-based platforms as alternative channels of communication to support their enterprises.

The central question of this book asks: Is social media empowering drug cartels in Mexico? The argument that guides this research is the claim that the adoption of social media is theorized to have a positive correlation with cartels' ability to survive. I hypothesized that those criminal organizations that have embraced social media usage strategically and with greater intensity have higher levels of survival capacity since these platforms allow for the dissemination of intelligence among cartel members, signal dominance to rivals, and allow for structural adaptation and the adoption of new organizational tactics.

The purpose of this work is twofold. The first is to fill in the gap in the literature by adding a new variable, *social media*, to the study of criminal organizations' survival capacity by offering a systematic study on the use of these communication platforms by the Mexican drug cartels, considered also to be transnational criminal organizations. The second purpose is to offer an alternative methodology to study the phenomenon, implementing social network analysis (SNA).

Surveying Criminal Organizations' Survival Capacity and Social Media Usage

In the pages that follow, this work demonstrates that some drug cartels in Mexico have incorporated social media into their strategies with the purpose of seeking new paths to dominance. It is important to highlight that this project does not imply causation. In other words, the study is not attempting to prove that social media causes a criminal organization's survival. Rather, the objective is to explore the effect it has on their level of survival capacity.

A cartel is defined here as an association of manufacturers or suppliers that regulate prices and purposely keep them high on a product to restrict competition. The Colombian drug cartels such as Cali and Medellín fitted this definition, for example. Criminal organizations in Mexico have diversified their criminal activities, and their *modus operandi* has evolved and adapted. In this context, the term "cartel" is no longer adequate to refer to Mexico's organized crime. In the drug trafficking literature, nevertheless, these terms are still widely applied. For this, the terms organized crime, criminal organizations, and drug cartels, are used interchangeably throughout this book.

The scope of this research covers the years from 2006 to 2015. To gain a deeper understanding of the effects of social media on drug cartels' survival, I conducted a comparative analysis of three criminal organizations. The cases explored in this study are: the Sinaloa cartel, the Zetas, and the Caballeros Templarios. A within-case analysis of these illegal organizations is attempted to draw an in-depth description of each case. More specifically, I examine each criminal organization through process tracing and structured focus comparison, a methodical tool used to identify stages in a causal process between the independent variables and the outcome (George & Bennett, 2005).

I selected these cases because they display variability in survival capacity and social media usage. All three organizations have experienced exogenous and internal blows; as a result of the variations, they differ in their type of response, level of adaptability, and ability to recover from organizational setbacks. Some of the groups present high rates of dispersion and growth and others have lost influence. Some have had resort to alliances; others have fragmented, and others have vanished. The cases also present different structural characteristics. This analysis progresses inductively to determine the ability or incapacity of the drug cartels to respond to organizational *shocks*, defined here as *events that can cause a disruption of the criminal organization* (Duijn, Kashirin, & Sloot, 2014). This type of events might have the ability to prevent the organizations from operating, or to slow down their decision-making process and reinforce their capabilities. The three criminal organizations are compared following the rationale of structured focus comparisons (George & Bennett, 2005).

The cases do not reflect an exhaustive list of all the drug cartels operating in Mexico. For instance, the number of criminal organizations in the country is hard to assess due to their constant fragmentation and re-amalgamation as new criminal groups. There are other cartels in Mexico such as the aforementioned Cartel Jalisco Nueva Generación, the Gulf cartel, the Tijuana, or the Beltrán Leyva, which are relevant players in the drug trafficking arena. These cases could add another layer of variation into my comparative analysis; nonetheless, some of those groups were either relatively young during the timeframe of my study, or had not widely adopted the technological or communications strategies presently seen in the drug business.

As discussed earlier, this work seeks to add a new variable to the study of criminal organizations' survival capacity. In order to understand the phenomenon, other variables such as the adoption of neoliberal regimes, or the opening of international markets, cartels' access to the U.S. consumer market, corruption, institutional weakness, government decentralization, party transition, and the profitability of the drug business, among others, cannot be ruled out.

Conceptualizing and Modeling Survival Capacity

This study aims to explain the capacity to survive of drug cartels facing aggressive state intervention. For the purpose of this analysis, *survival capacity* refers to *the ability of a system or network to adapt and keep functioning despite organizational setbacks*. The assessment of the criminal organizations' capacity to survive was conducted in two stages. First, a database on the cartels' confrontations was constructed. I collected data through archive research in *El Universal*.[4] The news items chosen to include in the datasets were reports of confrontations that explicitly implicated the cartel under study. Examining the actors with which each cartel battles gives a good indication of their symmetrical or asymmetrical capabilities compared to their rivals.

The second stage centers on organizational *shocks* or setbacks the cartels faced during the scope of this study. More specifically, the types of shocks analyzed are (i) *Mexican government military operations that led to the death or arrest of capos or an important leader*; (ii) *U.S. enforcement operations that led to the death or arrest of capos or an important leader*; (iii) *joint operations between the Mexican and U.S. government that led to the capture or death of capos or an important leader*; and (iv) *intra-cartel clashes that resulted in internal fragmentation, and the capture or killing of main leaders or capos*. Shocks are evaluated in a diachronic fashion since each criminal organization has received a different number of setbacks at different points in time.

According to Bakker, Raab, and Milward (2012), indicators of *survival capacity* can be depicted from the activities that make the criminal organization visible. I assessed the level of survival capacity by looking at the variations of: (i) *violence* (drug-related homicides), (ii) *criminal activities* (kidnappings and extortions). The indicators for adaptability are: (iii) *changes in their structure* and (iv) changes in their *modus operandi*.

Introduction 5

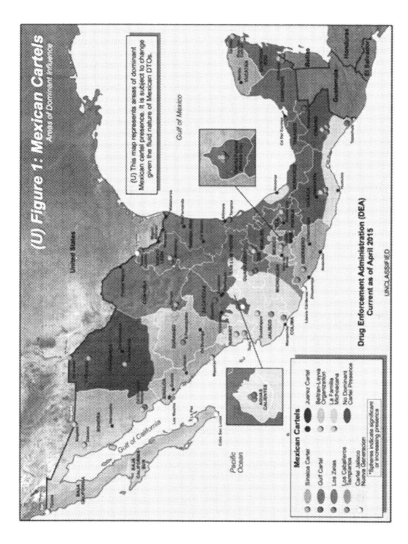

Map 0.1 Main Areas of Influence of the Major Mexican Drug Cartels.
Source: DEA (2015).

Data for drug-related homicides, kidnappings, and extortions, was surveyed from governmental institutions' reports from the Justice Attorney's Office (PGR) and INEGI (Instituto Nacional de Estadística y Geografía). I also examined archival data, secondary resources, scholarly journals, and national and international periodicals. To analyze major military operations and clashes between cartels and to select the most significant shocks for each criminal organization, I analyzed police reports and presidential speeches. It is important to highlight that the data available for this project presents limitations. The available databases present methodological concerns in regards to the categorization of drug-related homicides. The figures published by INEGI or PGR offer variations on the criteria for what constitutes a drug-related homicide (Correa-Cabrera & Nava, 2011). In addition, there are questions about the effectiveness of the official recognition of intentional homicide victims (Heinle, Rodríguez Ferreira, & Shirk, 2017). However, according to a special report from the University of San Diego, these two official data sources on intentional homicides in Mexico have been constantly documenting the data, and the general trends between these two sources are closely correlated (Heinle et al., 2017).

Social Media Usage Concepts, Data Gathering, and Social Network Analysis

The next phase of the analysis assesses the effect of social media utilization on the cartels' survival capacity. Social media usage is defined *as the criminal organization's ability to be present, active, and interactive on web-based social platforms, creating an effective footprint that allows them to have a base of fans and followers*. To evaluate the effect of social media use on criminal organizations, I explored three main platforms: Facebook, Twitter, and YouTube. I adapted each case study based on their usage, and the different platform preferences; this is explained in more detail in each corresponding chapter. To ensure anonymity when conducting content analysis, I created fake Facebook and Twitter accounts. From these accounts, I sent friend requests to members of the criminal organizations studied in this research in order to follow them and have access to their content. There was a personal account used to download data from NodeXL, the software I used to capture part of the Sinaloa cartel's Twitter network. NodeXL does not have the legal rights to do the same with Facebook accounts. For this reason, the databases of the Zetas' and Caballeros Templarios' Facebook networks were constructed manually, linking the accounts or nodes one by one and entering the information on a NodeXL spreadsheet to run several analyses. Map 0.1 shows the main areas of influence of the principal Mexican drug cartels during 2015.

I carried out the social media analysis in several stages. The first was to conduct a social network analysis on each case. A social network analysis is a helpful tool to visualize and uncover networked structures. A social network graph allows for the examination of the characteristics and dynamics of actors involved. It also serves to identify the nodes with higher degree centrality or clusters within a network (Garay Salamanca & Salcedo-Albarán, 2011: p. 40). In this study, a single point in the networks is considered a *node*. Each node represents an agent or individual that is part of the network. These nodes can be a cartel leader, members, rivals, politicians, civilians, journalists, or members of the Mexican and foreign security forces. The lines connecting two nodes are called *edges*. Edges indicate the social relationship between nodes. The arrangements of nodes and edges can be visualized in a *graph*, providing a general picture of the structure of a network (Otte & Rousseau, 2002).

To identify the most relevant nodes on the networks I used two main measures of centrality: *direct centrality* and *betweenness*. As Garay Salamanca and Salcedo-Albarán (2011) state: "In order to determine how relevant a node is for the potential conformation of a network, it is not enough to pay attention to the amount of connections; it is also necessary to evaluate the centrality indicator of betweenness" (p. 43).

The node with the highest degree of centrality is the one that concentrates the most connections with other nodes in the network. In this case, nodes with a high degree of centrality are the actors that have the most friends and followers on Twitter or Facebook. Central nodes hold a privileged position of influence within a network (Garay Salamanca & Salcedo-Albarán, 2011). These nodes with central positions can serve as disseminators of information. The second measure of centrality used in the study to identify the most relevant nodes in the social media networks is *betweenness*. Betweenness is conceptualized as a structural bridge. Although the nodes with high betweenness do not necessarily concentrate the greatest number of edges, these nodes connect the entire network together. They allow the flow of information where there is a structural hole, working as an arbitrator of the information and an intermediary on social relationships. In sum, calculating these two measures of centrality the indicators will identify: (i) the agent with the largest number of friends and followers on their Twitter or Facebook accounts, and (ii) the agent with the highest concentration of individual links.

Once I identified the accounts with high degrees of centrality and betweenness, I evaluated them under the following criteria to ensure veracity: (i) *the account shows clearly their association with a particular cartel*; (ii) *the person in the account declares a position within the organization* (e.g., sicario); (iii) *they tag other principal accounts related to an organization in posts and pictures*; (iv) *they show consistency in their content and context*; (v) *content of messages and images*; and (vi) *geographical positioning* (on the accounts that displayed it).

The analysis and data gathering on YouTube was slightly different. To find the videos that corresponded to each cartel, I directed a general search for the criminal organization through the platform's search engine. Later, I chose the *most relevant* filter and then studied the videos with more views and reproduction.

For the content analysis on the three platforms, I evaluated social media utilization in four dimensions: (i) presence, (ii) activity, (iii) purpose, and (iv) effectiveness. This variable was also monitored during: (i) the time between criminal organizational shocks; and (ii) the time before and after the signing of the media agreement to censor drug-related news in 2011. The indicators and criteria for presence and content analysis were chosen and applied depending on the information available on each platform. For example, on Facebook, in order to have access to an individual account, a "friend request" must be sent and should be accepted by the other party. On Twitter, information is more accessible by just "following" any account; nonetheless, each individual can apply a series of privacy settings. The content in YouTube is mostly open to the public. There are some restrictions on age when content is inappropriate to certain audiences.

Throughout the drug war years, the cartels have expanded and contracted all over the Mexican territory. For this, the data on violence and criminal activities which is used consists of the figures registered in the states in which the criminal organizations have had the most influence and the highest presence through time. These indicators are examined before and after major organizational disruptions. Each case study is different in that the periods of time under study vary; in other words, in some cases it was possible to monitor their activities before and after shocks for longer periods. This model is based on the study of dark network resilience by Bakker et al. (2012) and it has been modified for the purpose of this project. Figure 0.1 presents the model used for this study.

Following the model, I classified the case studies in three main categories, encompassing different levels of survival capacity: (i) *cartel that has remained dominant despite shocks* (high); (ii) *cartel that has been able to restore from shocks* (medium/high), evaluating also the time it took to restore; and (iii) *cartel with no ability to recover from shocks* (low).

This research faces some challenges, as the study of organized crime on social media is relatively new and there is no consensus on how to conduct it. Also, an important methodological concern with analyzing web-based communication platforms is that it is difficult to set up the boundaries of the network; this is the "boundary specification problem" or problem of "fuzzy boundaries," which suggests that the borders of a network can be unclear (Duijn et al., 2014; Sparrow, 1991). There is also the concern of account authenticity, which this study attempts to minimize following the criteria presented earlier.

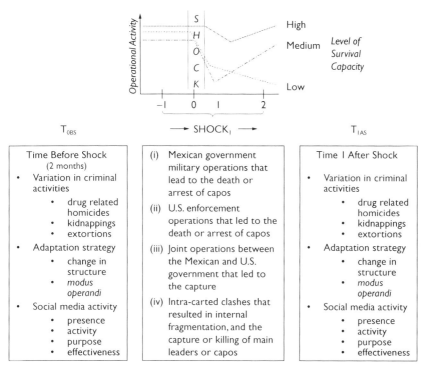

Figure 0.1 Survival Capacity of Criminal Organizations and Social Media Usage Model.

Organization of the Book

This book is divided into three parts. The first part (Chapters 1 and 2) provides an overview of the rise of the Mexican drug cartels and presents an examination of the role of the media in the conflict. Chapter 1 has three core foci. It begins with a brief account of the historic legacies that contributed to the rise of some of the most powerful and dangerous drug cartels in the world. Then, the chapter turns to a discussion of the evolution of the war on drugs in Mexico from 2006 to 2015, describing the transition of the military strategies and drug policy from the Calderón to Peña Nieto's administration. Finally, I shift the focus to a discussion of the analytical approaches that aims to explain the Mexican drug cartels' capacity for survival.

Chapter 2 explores the role the media has played in Mexico's drug war, highlighting the transition from traditional approaches to the adoption of social media as a major source of information about the drug war by civilians, and cartels. This chapter also surveys the analytical approaches that have studied the usage and effects of social media by criminal organizations or terrorist groups such as ISIS and criminal organizations in Mexico.

The second part consists of three chapters (Chapters 3 to 5); each presents a case study of a particular cartel. Chapter 3 introduces the Sinaloa cartel. Better known for its infamous leader Joaquín "El Chapo" Guzmán, the Sinaloa cartel is one of the largest and most powerful drug trafficking organizations in the world. In this study, the organization is considered a traditional drug cartel.[5] This criminal group has a significant presence on social media. Just on Twitter, the Sinaloa cartel's network has more than 140 million followers combined. The social network analysis of their Twitter network reveals a similar structure to the one the organization holds physically (i.e., hub-and-spokes),[6] it also exposes some dynamics and characteristics of the cartel. That is, some structural and behavioral patterns can be depicted, such as subgroups and personal interests. This case presented the most successful social media strategy out of the three criminal groups. The Sinaloa approach focuses on (i) social acceptance; (ii) use of social media as a force multiplier; and (iii) establishment of a closed–open communication system in which the most central nodes serve as information disseminators. Although, throughout the drug war years, the cartel has suffered significant disruptions, the most important one being the capture of El Chapo, the organization presents the highest level of survival capacity in this study. The cartel has been able to maintain its hegemony among Mexican drug cartels.

Employing the same analytical approach, Chapter 4 focuses on the Zetas cartel. The Zetas is a criminal organization that transformed the drug trafficking business in Mexico. Here, it is considered a "non-traditional" cartel. This group originated in the state of Tamaulipas, and emerged from the Gulf cartel, for which members served as the armed wing until 2008–2009. The Zetas are better known for their hyper-violence and the brutal ways in which they conduct their business. They are also known for the rapid growth and significant territorial expansion achieved at the height of their power, around 2010 and 2012. The Zetas' Facebook social network analysis exhibits a complex decentralized network. The examination shows that their level of decentralization gives roots for additional subnetworks to emerge mimicking their physical structures. In this case, the early detection of emerging cells was possible: this study shows glimpses of the Cartel del Noreste developing. The Zetas social media presence is not as prominent as that of the Sinaloa cartel. Nevertheless, they follow a specific strategy: *psychological warfare*. They use social media mostly to incite terror and send threatening messages. The Zetas' aggressive approach on social media has been effective and resulted in them dominating and controlling through fear. The leaders of the organization maintain a low profile and do not have public accounts as do El Chapo and other Sinaloa cartel leaders such Alfredo and Ivan Archivaldo Guzmán. This case showed no evidence that the utilization of social media by this cartel has contributed to their exposure or more targeting. On the contrary, the analysis indicates that its usage has benefited the organization. This case also showed that social media could become the Achilles' heel for criminal organizations as the Zetas showed vulnerability when facing attacks from civilians. Though the Zetas have retreated from some territories, and splintered into the Zetas Old School and Cartel del Noreste, they remain a relevant cartel in the drug trafficking scene in the hemisphere. The context under which social media usage functions within the Zetas' domains has unfolded differently from that in the regions where the Sinaloa cartel operates. The underlying character of the virtual interactions between the Zetas, the authorities, and the citizens, has created an unprecedented situation, altering in a way the dynamics of the conflict, in which the citizens have become yet another actor in the war on drugs. The fight, it seems, has become a multi-level battle of all against all.

Chapter 5 focuses on the Caballeros Templarios cartel. Based mainly in the state of Michoacán, this criminal organization had its origins in the Familia Michoacana, the third most powerful cartel in Mexico before its collapse in 2010. The Caballeros Templarios, like the Zetas, display a non-traditional *modus operandi*. Compared to the other cases, the cartel's social media presence is at the medium level. The Caballeros Templarios present a different social media platform preference, offering a clear example of the *social media paradox*. Although this organization is also present on Facebook, their main leader at the time, Servando Gómez "La Tuta," preferred to use YouTube. The former leader uploaded a series of videos that might have led to his capture. Compared to the other two cases presented in this book, the analysis in this chapter finds that the social media strategy followed by La Tuta was not effective. Although their Facebook exposure does not seem to have had negative effects on the organization, it is La Tuta's usage of YouTube that shows harmful repercussions. In this case, the correlation between social media usage and reported clashes was statistically significant, meaning that the over exposure on YouTube, due to the nature of the platform, contributed to an increase in their targeting, leading to the capture of their leader. After La Tuta's incarceration, the cartel eventually dismantled.

The third part concludes this book. The conclusion closes by presenting the main theoretical and empirical findings, prospects for future research, and a discussion of the redefining of the concept of drug cartels and criminal organizations. It also assesses the evolution of the conflict; the drug policy presented by Andrés Manuel López Obrador, the re-accommodation of criminal organizations during most recent years, and, finally, the present and current challenges of the drug conflict.

Summary of Findings and Conclusion

I find that the strategic adaptation of social media platforms has different effects on criminal organizations' ability to survive. The empirical evidence suggests that, if used efficiently, social media is a tool that benefits and strengthens drug cartels in Mexico, by enhancing both their organizational and operational capabilities. I propose that, when used effectively, and coupled with the adoption of decentralized structures, these platforms do increase criminal organizations' survival capacity. If used haphazardly, they can have the opposite effect. Social media strengthens criminal organizations mainly by enhancing their legitimacy and attracting new recruits. Measuring how much legitimacy or at what rate social media attracts recruits, thereby increasing the survival capacity of drug cartels, is hard. The statistical correlation analysis suggests that, contrary to the arguments of various scholars, in the case of the Sinaloa cartel and the Zetas, there is no compelling evidence indicating that their exposure on social media made them more vulnerable to attacks by rivals or the government.

By using social network analysis, this research gathered a great deal of information about drug cartels, providing fresh insights regarding their organizational networks, their central nodes, and the channels through which information flows in these criminal groups. Through my analysis, I found that in the cases of the Sinaloa cartel and the Zetas, their virtual network was reminiscent of their physical structure. I also found that early detection of emerging cells within the structures of the criminal organizations is possible. From the vantage point of policy and intelligence, the detection of nascent cells is of significance for two reasons. First, it allows for their identification and targeting, before they become independent and powerful cartels. Second, it might signal intra-cartel fragmentation, indicating vulnerability. Furthermore, the content of the social media platforms analyzed in this study reveals the cartels' strategies, tactics, demographics, and information about real-time operations.

Social media has become a central outlet in which members of criminal organizations provide great amounts of information, which, in turn, offers alternative perspectives that can contribute to the understanding of these groups. This work seeks to add a new variable to the study of cartels' survival capacity. Furthermore, it proposes the implementation of social network analysis in the study of drug cartels as a tool to investigate the nature of the "new networked generation" of criminal organizations.

Social media is treated in this book as an alternative variable to explain the survival capacity of criminal organizations in Mexico. It is worth mentioning that there are other variables that might have also strong explanatory power, such as the economic flux of the criminal organizations, their military capabilities, or intelligence capacity. Approaching this topic is imperative, since the effect of social media as a tool used by criminal networks in Mexico remains understudied. Proven significant, this variable might be extrapolated to the study of additional cases within Mexico and of criminal organizations in Colombia, Brazil, or El Salvador.

Notes

1 Social media is defined here as websites and applications that enable users to create and share content or to participate in social networking. See: https://en.oxforddictionaries.com/definition/social_media (accessed 2017).
2 The criteria are available at: http://expansion.mx/nacional/2011/03/24/medios-mexicanos-firman-un-acuerdo-para-informar-sobre-violencia.
3 In 2000, only 5 percent of the Mexican population had access to the internet. By 2010, one-third had access to it. As of June 2012, more than 33 million people, 30 percent of the population, had Facebook accounts, ranking fifth in the world in the number of Facebook users. Information available at Internet World Stats: www.internetworldstats.com/central.htm#mx.
4 *El Universal* was chosen as the main source to get the data on confrontations for several reasons. This new journal has national coverage in Mexico, and has been one of the newspapers with higher circulation regarded as a reliable, trustworthy source of news. In 2001, the newspaper launched its website that covers the content of the newspaper, and it added new multimedia sections. *El Universal*'s portal is one of the most visited Spanish-speaking news outlets worldwide, with 507,000 users logging in a day, and 5.2 million visits per month. Although *El Universal* was one of the media outlets to sign the media initiative discussed in the previous chapter, the journal has established its own code of ethics when covering organized crime, maintaining that it is still its responsibility to diffuse truthful information about the drug war and to promote denunciation by civil society but without advocating violence. The criteria *El Universal* follows are available at: www.eluniversal.com.mx/criterios-ante-violencia.
5 The terms "traditional cartels" and "non-traditional cartels" are used in this work to refer to the organizations' *modus operandi*. For example, the Sinaloa cartel is considered "traditional" because it has for the most part maintained the tacit agreements followed by the Mexican cartels for decades: (1) protect the communities in which they operate, (2) do not to kill innocent civilians, (3) respect rival cartels' turf, and (4) generate their profits mainly from drug trafficking activities. More recently, there have been indicators that the cartel is departing from the traditional ways; these will be discussed later in this book. "Non-traditional" cartels refer to more recently established criminal organizations such as the Zetas, La Familia, the Caballeros Templarios, and the Cartel Jalisco Nueva Generación. These newer groups do not follow the "rules of the game" and use violent, indiscriminate tactics to conduct their illegal businesses.
6 In a "hub-and-spokes" structure typology the leadership of the organization is shared by various individuals. In the case of the Sinaloa cartel the organization started with four main leaders, each working with their own cells and groups, and enjoying some degree of autonomy (Astorga, 1999).

References

Astorga, L. (1999). *Drug trafficking in Mexico: A first general assessment*. Management of Social Transformations MOST. United Nations Educational, Scientific and Cultural Organization Discussion Paper No. 36.

Bakker, R. M., Raab, J., & Milward, H. B. (2012). A preliminary theory of dark network resilience. *Journal of Policy Analysis and Management*, 31(1), 33–62.

Calderón, L., Heinle, K., Rodríguez Ferreira, O., & Shirk, D. A. (2019). *Organized crime and violence in Mexico: Analysis through 2018*. Justice in Mexico. Department of Political Science and International Relations University of San Diego.

Retrieved from: https://justiceinmexico.org/wp-content/uploads/2019/04/Organized-Crime-and-Violence-in-Mexico-2019.pdf.

Correa-Cabrera, G., & Nava, J. (2011). *Drug wars, social networks and the right to information: The rise of informal media as the freedom of press's lifeline in northern Mexico*. APSA 2011 Annual Meeting Paper.

Duijn, P. A., Kashirin, V., & Sloot, P. M. (2014). The relative ineffectiveness of criminal network disruption. *Scientific Reports, 4*, 4238.

Garay Salamanca, L. J., & Salcedo-Albarán, E. (2011). *Drug trafficking corruption and states. How illicit networks reconfigure institutions in Colombia, Guatemala and Mexico*. Bogotá, Colombia: Fundación Método.

George, A. L., & Bennett, A. (2005). *Case studies and theory development in the social sciences*. Cambridge, MA: MIT Press.

Heinle, K., Rodríguez Ferreira, O., & Shirk, D. A. (2017). *Drug violence in Mexico. Data and analysis through 2016*. Justice in Mexico. Special Report. University of San Diego.

Otte, E., & Rousseau, R. (2002). Social network analysis: A powerful strategy, also for the information sciences. *Journal of Information Science, 28*(6), 441–453.

Sparrow, M. K. (1991). The application of network analysis to criminal intelligence: An assessment of the prospects. *Social Networks, 13*, 251–274.

Chapter 1

Narco Mexico

Felipe Calderón militarized the "war on drugs" in Mexico in 2006. This drug policy approach has generated high rates of violence, bloody confrontations between cartels and security forces, and preeminent levels of collateral damage, all of which still plague the country today. As of 2018, the atrocities of the drug war have led to more than 332,000 homicides, excluding a significant number of disappearances, and undocumented killings (Calderón et al., 2019). Thousands of civilians and families have also suffered human rights violations at the hands of the military. According to the Mexican Commission for the Defense and Promotion of Human Rights, the number of civilians misplaced in Mexico during the conflict is more than 310,000 (Fregoso, 2017). In addition, entire communities across Mexico, such as San Luis de la Loma in Guerrero, Chilapa in Sinaloa, or Ciudad Mier in the state of Tamaulipas, just to mention a few, have become ghost towns, abandoned due to the vicious abuses from criminal organizations (Fregoso, 2017). The strategy implemented by the government throughout this conflict against drug trafficking has not proven successful; there is a metastasis of criminal organizations in the country, some of them have maintained or have gained more power, drugs are still crossing borders, consumption is rising worldwide, violence is spiking, and the bloodshed in Mexico seems endless.

This chapter presents a brief account of the war on drugs in Mexico, its origins and evolution. It also explores the securitization of the war and discusses the strategies taken by the administration of Felipe Calderón (2006–2012) and Peña Nieto (2012–2016) to combat organized crime, assessing their successes, failures, and challenges. Finally, the chapter presents different theories that attempt to explain Mexican cartels' power and survival capacity.

Drug Trafficking in Mexico: Before and After Militarization

While the speed and brutal violence with which the drug trafficking phenomenon took over Mexico during the last decade is surprising, the existence of criminal organizations involved with drugs is not. Historically, Mexico has been a producer of marijuana, opium, and heroin. This remained for many years a regionally based activity (Andreas, 2009). Mexico has also served as a transit country for cocaine from other parts of South America, such as the Andean region, especially Colombia. The country has the geographic, social, cultural, and political conditions to make the drug business functional and lucrative, contributing to the proliferation of criminal insurgency (Grillo, 2011). Bordering the biggest and most profitable drug market in the world, the U.S., places Mexico in a desirable location to conduct the illegal business. In addition, the state's institutional capacity is weak due to high levels of corruption deeply rooted in the system and evidenced by long-standing established relationships between government authorities and organized crime (Astorga, 2004; Valdés Castellanos, 2013; Grayson, 2014; Rios, 2012).

In other words, the problem of drug trafficking in Mexico is anything but new. Tacit and informal agreements between state and drug cartels were established many years ago under the PRI (Institutional Revolutionary Party) regime that ruled the country for 71 years (Astorga, 2005; Valdés Castellanos, 2013). During the PRI's hegemony, however, there was a sense of relative peace and stability in the way drug cartels operated (Carvajal-Dávila, 1998). According to Astorga (2005), the agreements established between the PRI and the drug cartels rested on a specific understanding on the part of the government. The arrangement entailed the following points: (i) illicit drugs were destined just for export and not for domestic consumption; (ii) cartel members, or capos, would not seek political participation; and (iii) decisions taken by the federal government would be obeyed without disputes (Snyder & Duran-Martinez, 2009; Duran-Martinez, 2018). Under this system, drug trafficking organizations coexisted and functioned in a well-ordered fashion, maintaining their operations without major violent confrontations among themselves or with the government.

The Mexican drug cartels began to become notorious during the 1960s, a decade that saw an explosion in the demand for marijuana in the U.S. This was the era of the Vietnam War and the hippie generation. Marijuana became the symbol of youthful rebellion and political dissent. During the following years, the consumption trend started to change in the northern country, increasing the demand for cocaine. In the 1980s, the U.S. interdiction efforts along the Florida coast resulted in the closing of trafficking routes through the Caribbean. This policy altered drug trafficking paths to the U.S., shifting them to Mexico and the Pacific corridor (Freeman & Sierra, 2005). As a result, Colombian cartels started to establish a strong nexus with the Mexican cartels (i.e., Guadalajara with Pablo Escobar's Medellín cartel, and the Gulf with the Cali cartel), to traffic cocaine, making the illicit industry even more successful and profitable. Longtime marijuana smugglers in Mexico became part of a complex and more sophisticated hemispheric network of drug traffickers, increasing their influence and power (Astorga, 2004). After the demise of the Colombian cartels, Mexican cartels and capos, such as Félix Gallardo known as "El Padrino" (the Godfather), became influential figures in the international arena of the drug business (Grayson, 2014), filling the vacuum left in Colombia and taking over the drug industry in the Americas.

As a neoliberal agenda dominated the Western world, Mexico signed the North American Free Trade Agreement (NAFTA), formalized in 1994 during the presidency of Carlos Salinas de Gortari. With the opening of the U.S., Canadian, and Mexican borders for trade, it became more challenging for the authorities to control the crossing of illegal substances through the Mexican–American frontier. Ultimately, NAFTA created the conditions for cartels to expand their operations (Gootenberg, 2011; Astorga, 2010; Eiss, 2014; Bagley, 2005; Andreas, 2009).

The signing of NAFTA carried some other unintended consequences. On the one hand, foreign investment benefited the country in some sectors. The *maquiladoras* established in border cities offered numerous job opportunities, especially for women. Also, multinational corporations started founding headquarters in industrial cities, stimulating their economies. On the other hand, domestic production of agricultural products, especially in the southern part of the country, failed to get the protection blanket needed to survive the international competition (McKibben, 2015). The latter led to problems with growers and Mexico witnessing the rise of the *Ejército Zapatista de Liberación Nacional* (EZLN), a paramilitary group with socialist and Marxist ideals. They were fighting against the adoption of the neoliberal establishment. The rebels claimed that the collective rights historically belonging to the indigenous communities had been neglected by foreign investment and competition, making these communities unable to compete with foreign markets and generating more poverty and greater inequality. The economic divergence pushed some of these communities to look for other means of income and they turned to the drug trafficking business (McKibben, 2015). The lack of job opportunities in the formal sector, in particular for the underqualified and poorly educated, broadened the workforce willing to participate in the illicit industry.

In 2000, democracy took a stand in Mexico when Vicente Fox, the candidate from the opposition party PAN (National Action Party), won the federal election. After Fox's election, the geopolitics of drug trafficking in Mexico began to shift almost imperceptibly until a new reality struck the country (Aguilar & Castañeda, 2009). The rules of the game changed, and the agreements between drug cartels and the PRI that had functioned for generations were shattered. Nineteen years later, the drug trafficking panorama is completely transformed, new political parties dominate different regions, and the agreements have been reestablished with different cartels. During this restructuring process and re-accommodation of turf and power, violence has permeated the country. As Williams (2009) puts it, "Mexico ... suffers from transitional violence (arrangements for criminal activity which were dominated by the state have broken down), [is] characterized by anomie and a culture of lawlessness ... and [is] afflicted by high levels of corruption" (p. 326). This, coupled with the social embeddedness of the narco culture in Mexico (Sullivan & Bunker, 2011; Sullivan, 2012), has brought together the exact elements needed to create the perfect storm.

The Securitization of the War on Drugs

To understand the securitization of the drug war in Mexico, it is important to consider the political context in which Felipe Calderón took office in 2006. Calderón started his administration amidst electoral chaos. A significant percentage of the population believed Andrés Manuel López Obrador (AMLO) or "El Peje," the candidate, at that time, for the leftist PRD (Democratic Revolutionary Party), and now the president of Mexico, was the legitimate winner. Those who contested the 2006 presidential election argued that Obrador received more of the votes, claiming electoral fraud on the part of Calderón (Resendiz, 2006).[1]

The political turmoil led scholars to debate whether the lack of acceptance of his mandate was an important factor that influenced Calderón's decision to militarize the drug conflict, as a desperate effort to gain the nation's approval (Aguilar & Castañeda, 2009). What differentiates Calderón's approach to drug trafficking *vis-à-vis* his predecessors is that no former president launched such an aggressive and permanent strategy, involving the military instead of the federal police to fight organized crime (Aguilar & Castañeda, 2009; Carpenter, 2012). In his rhetoric, Calderón highlighted the indispensability of the military forces to fight the cartels. Often, during televised discourses, he stated that the battle was essential to stop drugs from reaching Mexican children (Carreño de la Rosa, 2011). He framed the problem of drug trafficking and the cartels as the number one threat to the country's national security, claiming that domestic drug consumption was increasing dramatically and that cartels were threatening to subvert the government.

Even though the drug war was successfully securitized, the justifications offered by the Mexican government have been strongly contested by experts. Figures have shown that drug consumption in Mexico might be rising, but the increase is neither significant nor alarming. The argument that the drug trafficking organizations were attempting to displace the government has been totally refuted by specialists, who have documented that Mexican cartels have never exhibited an intent to do so (Aguilar & Castañeda, 2009). Finally, violence has not decreased with the persecution of cartels; on the contrary, the Mexican territory has become a massive graveyard.

Sharing Responsibilities: the Merida Initiative

It is regularly argued that Mexico's drug trafficking problem is a demand-side issue, stemming from high levels of drug consumption in the U.S. In a meeting to discuss the drug problem with former president George W. Bush in Guatemala, Felipe Calderón proclaimed, "while there is no reduction in demand in your territory, it will be very difficult to reduce the supply in ours" (as cited in Grayson, 2014: p. 93). With this statement, the Mexican president urged Washington to "share responsibilities" and support Mexico in addressing the anti-drug effort (Grayson, 2014).

In response to Calderón's challenge, the Merida Initiative was signed in 2007 by the Mexican and American presidents. This approach mirrored the model of *Plan Colombia*, led by the U.S. during the Colombian war on drugs fought during the late 1900s. The U.S. Congress agreed to fund the Merida Initiative with $1.4 billion for training, equipment, justice sector reforms, police capacity building, intelligence and anti-corruption programs (Grayson, 2014). Cutrona (2017) refers to this approach as the *Standard Security Model* (SSM) imposed by the U.S. throughout Latin America and the Caribbean for counter-narcotic efforts. He defines the model as:

> A set of policies that promotes the expansion of the military's role in counter-narcotics efforts, applied irrespective of the nature of the target country's drug problem. Underpinned by a harsh counter-narcotics legislation, this model provides aid grants for security purposes; the training of armed and civilian police forces in military operation and strategies; advice, intelligence, and logistical support; and the transfer of weapons, equipment, and services to fight against drug-trafficking. Most important, the SSM frames the drug problem as one analogous to traditional national security preoccupations, often overlooking its economic, social, and cultural dimensions.

The SSM has been the common approach to combat drug trafficking in various South American countries such as Colombia, Bolivia, and Peru. The strategy has been highly disputed by scholars and experts as to its effectiveness versus the adverse consequences of its implementations. Some examples cover the negative environmental impact, the pollution of lakes and rivers, as well as soil degradation caused by the spraying of chemicals to eradicate poppy or coca leaves crops.

In addition, the scheme implemented follows the "kingpin" strategy, which consists in high-value targeting; in other words, it intends to cripple a criminal organization through "decapitation," capturing or killing the main leader or leaders. The logic behind this strategy is that by taking away the head of the organization, the criminal group will splinter into smaller, weaker groups that are easier to defeat. The kingpin approach proved successful in dismantling the hierarchically structured Cali and Medellín cartels in Colombia, the most powerful Latin American criminal organizations at the time (Bakker et al., 2012; Duran-Martinez, 2018). However, this strategy has not shown the same satisfactory results against Mexican cartels.

The Merida Initiative never took off as expected. After the attacks of 9/11, the U.S.'s military interests shifted towards Afghanistan, and the War on Terror escalated to the top of the U.S. security agenda. Terrorists groups such as Al Qaeda and the Taliban became a major threat to the American national security. The "war on drugs" declared by President Nixon in 1971 was supplanted by the "war on terror" under George W. Bush's mandate. The fight against drug trafficking was no longer a priority to the U.S. What is more, the economic recession and health-care legislation, and the Mexican military's notorious and repeated violation of human rights, are accounted as some of the factors that influenced the U.S. Congress's decision of limiting the allocation of resources to the Merida Initiative, hurting its chances of success (Grayson, 2014).

During the drug war years, some Mexican cartels have proven to be highly resistant. Regardless of the setbacks, the Merida Initiative did have some impact on the criminal organizations. Constant government harassment of the cartels has led to both the *balloon* and the *cockroach* effects (explained below), along with the shifting of drug trafficking routes back to Colombia and to parts of Central America and the Caribbean (Bagley, 2012). Looking for safe havens to conduct their operations, and taking advantage of the increase of consumption in other regions of the world (i.e., Europe and West Africa), some of the Mexican cartels have established their illegal activities in other countries. They are creating transnational networks with criminal organizations and gangs in Central America such as MS-13 and Barrio 18. Central American countries suffer from fragile governments and institutions, which creates protection rackets that benefit organized crime (Kassab & Rosen, 2019). In addition, such networks and criminal cells are expanding through the rest of the continent and close ties are forming between Mexican cartels and criminal organization in countries in the southern cone, such as Brazil.

From Calderón (2006–2012) to Peña Nieto (2012–2018)

The PRI found its way back to *Los Pinos* with President Peña Nieto in 2012, and during his administration they handled the drug war narrative a bit differently from his predecessor. To begin with, the term "Merida Initiative" vanished from the official discourse. During his mandate, the former president turned his statements away from the conflict, focusing more on economic issues and energy reforms. As if the war on drugs had ended, silence remained his main approach (Ramos, 2013).

Yet, in some instances, it was impossible for him to ignore the ongoing crisis. For example, President Peña Nieto addressed the nation in regards to the disappearance of a group of young civilians from Ayotzinapa, Guerrero. In September 26, 2014, a group of 43 male teaching college students went missing in the town of Iguala. Supposedly, the students were taken by local authorities, and were never seen again. Five years later, their disappearance remains unsolved. There are suspicions and theories that indicate the future teachers ended up in the hands of members of a criminal organization who later killed them (Franco, 2018; Melesio, 2019). The tragedy still haunts Mexican society and brings to light many issues such as the high levels of impunity, the targeting of innocent civilians, the state–criminal organizations nexus, injustice, and the suffering of innocent people. The former president made another statement related to the drug war when "El Chapo" Guzmán tunneled out of jail (for the second time), after having been in prison for only six months. Peña Nieto was in Paris celebrating France's Independence Day, accompanied by more than 100 members of the Mexican military and cadets parading through the Champs Élysées. From there, he broadcasted a short communiqué listing the immediate actions his government would take to recapture Guzmán. He later delivered a brief speech celebrating the "triumph" of the government over the Sinaloa cartel with El Chapo's arrest in January of 2016. After these happenings, he made only sporadic declarations about El Chapo's extradition process to the U.S., completed in January of 2017.

From the beginning of his administration, Peña Nieto was extremely critical of Calderón's militarized approach to combat drug trafficking. Nonetheless, the fundamentals of the anti-drug strategy remained largely the same. One novelty in Peña Nieto's tactics was the creation of a military force called *La Gendarmería Nacional*, modeled after France's gendarmerie and the national police of several South American countries. The group was supposed to replace more than 40,000 troops (Althaus, 2013). In addition, the former president adopted a more arm's-length relationship with the U.S. officials from the Drug Enforcement Administration (DEA) and other agencies, which had worked closely with the previous administration (Althaus, 2013).

A Critical State of Affairs

After more than a decade of constant conflict, the war on drugs has taken a turn for the worse. Cartels have multiplied and others fragmented creating *cartelitos*. A considerable number of new and more violent cartels arose in different areas of Mexico. There are records of nine cartels and 113 drug trafficking cells currently operating in the country. These groups also exhibit more compartmentalization and have diversified their criminal activities to include kidnappings, extortions, human trafficking, and oil theft (Garay Salamanca & Salcedo-Albarán, 2011). Some cartels, such as the Zetas, have grown exponentially in size and power, gaining control over more territory (Dudley & Rios, 2013) and later retracted. In 2011, the *Cartel Jalisco Nueva Generación* joined the drug trafficking scene, and, presently, is considered one of the most powerful criminal organizations and the main rival to the Sinaloa cartel. As this cartel gets stronger, other major groups have shrunk in power and capabilities (e.g., La Familia Michoacana). Prior to 2010, drug cartels mainly operated in ten states in the Republic; however, there has been a metastasis of criminal cells throughout the entire territory (Santos, 2014). What is more, according to a 2017 United Nations report, Mexico has the third-largest areas of poppy cultivation worldwide (after Afghanistan and Myanmar) (United Nations Office on Drugs and Crime, 2017). The country is also a global leader in the trafficking of chemical precursors needed to produce methamphetamines.

The drug war fiasco can be attributed to problems in its execution and coordination, and a lack of transparency from law enforcement bodies; and to desynchronization at the municipal, state, and federal levels. There are instances in which violent clashes take place between the military and the municipal police forces, instead of fighting criminals together. Events like these illustrate the failure in communication among the law enforcement agencies. A course of action taken by the federal government to minimize the inconsistencies was the implementation of *Mando Unico*, which aimed to centralize the security forces at the state level and regain the ability to work as a cohesive, single decision-making body.

The multi-level, uncoordinated judicial system has been unable to control the criminal arena in Mexico; experts correlate the latter to a recent upsurge of violence in the country and the inability to fight now fragmented and dispersed criminal organizations (Rios, 2018). As Rios (2018) posits "[t]oday's crisis is the result of changes in the *modus operandi* of criminals that are not mirrored by changes in Mexico's judicial and police institutions" (p. 1). It is important to consider that the main constitutional purpose of the Mexican army is to guard and protect the national sovereignty from external threats. Their training, logistics, equipment, and command structure are not designed to deal with the investigation of crimes; they do not know how to properly navigate the judicial system, or how to process a criminal to the proper jurisdiction. The military forces in Mexico are experiencing attrition and loss of confidence among some sectors of the population due to repressive actions or police functions, which they have no formal training to perform (Gobierno de Mexico, 2019). The militarization of the conflict in Mexico has brought other serious consequences such as the increase of human rights violations.

Mexican Drug Cartels' Survival Capacity

After a decade of constant targeting, and persecution not only by the Mexican military, but also by the U.S. government (the highest-level military force in the world), and after the regular battles with rival cartels for turf, criminal organizations in Mexico continue to operate; new criminal organizations have appeared, and others like the Sinaloa cartel have become even more powerful. What makes the Mexican drug cartels so resistant?

There are various ways of categorizing the existing models and theoretical frameworks that have approached this question. Prolific works are situated at the transnational, national, and structural levels of analysis. Here these factors are organized under three main bodies of inquiry: (i) exogenous factors, (ii) domestic dynamics, and (iii) the internal structural topology of criminal organizations. A more detailed examination of the contending explanations of what makes Mexico ideal for drug trafficking and a breeder of some of the most powerful criminal organizations in the world is provided in this section.

Exogenous Factors

In the drug trafficking literature, two classic paradigms that have tried to explain the consolidation of the illicit business in some Latin American countries point to external forces. As this section further elaborates, some authors argue that globalization and the adoption of neoliberal regimes opened new opportunities that facilitated the proliferation of the drug trade. Others attribute the phenomena to the U.S. involvement in drug policy in the Americas.

The Opening of Borders

Criminal organizations benefit from the increasingly globalized international system. As Bagley (2005) suggests, these groups have taken advantage of the opening of borders, the liberalization of immigration policies, the spread of technology, and the under-regulation of international financial network globalization. This has eased the development of more sophisticated drug trafficking organizations.

From an international relations perspective, some scholars believe that the adoption of neoliberal regimes provided fertile ground for organized crime to flourish in Latin America (Gootenberg, 2011). As previously discussed, experts propose that the signing of NAFTA in 1994, by the U.S., Canada, and Mexico, contributed to the strengthening of drug trafficking in the region (Gootenberg, 2011; Astorga, 2010; Eiss, 2014).

The adoption of NAFTA also reinforced the coexistence of the formal and informal economy that the drug business generates (Andreas, 2009). This is possible due to the unfeasibility of grasping control over all the commodities crossing over the U.S.–Mexico 3,145 km border. Trade between the two countries amounted to $671 billion in 2018, and more than 250,000 vehicles cross daily (Office of the United States Trade Representative, 2019; Freeman & Sierra, 2005). The impacts of NAFTA are paradoxical, Andreas (2009) argues, as the treaty has led to the creation of "a borderless economy and a barricaded border" (p. 1). In other words, the trade agreement between the two nations allows for the free flow of goods, but at the same time, such openness eases the trade of illegal substances.

In terms of policy, criminal organizations in Mexico also deal with border enforcement operations. In that respect, some scholars observe that in running such operations, the U.S. is only supporting a self-reinforcing cycle for these groups (Andreas, 2009; Schendel & Abraham, 2005). According to Andreas (2003) when states' pressure on the borders is high, criminal organizations adopt a *double-funnel model*. Under this model, he suggests, the number of trafficking organizations will decrease, but their sophistication will increase. Similarly, Schendel and Abraham (2005) concluded that criminal organizations confronting such conditions are forced to adapt, and have adopted new technologies to become more specialized in their methods for trafficking illicit goods across the border, giving them more leverage.

The U.S.-Led War on Drugs

The prohibitionist drug regime in the United States can be traced back to the passing of the Harrison Narcotics Tax Act in 1914. It evolved into a more repressive paradigm during the 1970s and 1980s when the country experienced an outburst of crack cocaine consumption (Youngers & Rosin, 2005; Isacson, 2005; Carpenter, 2003). President Richard Nixon declared the "war on drugs" in 1971, acknowledging drugs as an existential threat; since then, the U.S. has been actively involved in anti-drug efforts in the world, more specifically in Latin America and the Caribbean. Years later, and concerned about the ongoing social and economic consequences of the drug problem, President Reagan took an even harsher policy line, urging the militarization of the counter-narcotic fight (Youngers & Rosin, 2005; Tokatlian & Bagley, 2007).

Youngers and Rosin (2005) examined the impact of the U.S.-led war on drugs in various Latin American countries. They found that the impositions of the U.S. paradigm have not proven successful at eradicating crops or minimizing consumption. Rather, the approach has brought unintended consequences that in many cases have stimulated the drug industry even more. For example, the approach triggered the "balloon effect" which consists in the shifting of coca leaf production from one region to another. In 2000, coca cultivation in Peru and Bolivia declined significantly due to the eradication strategies, but it shifted to Colombia, making it the main source country producing 90 percent of the world's cocaine (Bagley, 2012; Loveman, 2006; Youngers & Rosin; 2005; Gootenberg, 2011). Another outcome is the "cockroach effect," referring to the dispersion, fragmentation, and displacement of criminal organizations from one region to another within a given country or across borders. Such dispersion has been especially visible in the cases of Colombia and Mexico (Bagley, 2012; Gootenberg; 2011). In addition, one more inadvertent result has been the shifting of smuggling routes (Bagley, 2012). Additional collateral damage associated with the U.S.-led war on drugs in Latin American countries includes: high rates of violence, prison overpopulation, environmental degradation, deeper corruption among local police forces, human rights violations, the erosion of democracy, and worsened economic conditions in some regions (Youngers & Rosin, 2005; Loveman, 2006; Andreas & Nadelmann, 2006).

Due to the broadly documented negative impacts of the war on drugs, the delegitimization of the prohibitionist model has grown among Latin American and Caribbean governments (Youngers & Rosin, 2005; Loveman, 2006; Andreas & Nadelmann, 2006). Nonetheless, despite its acknowledged ineffectiveness, the model remains enforced in many countries, including Mexico.

Domestic Dynamics

The domestic conditions in a country in which criminal organizations operate can play a role in their demise or their growth. Scholarship in criminology and political science has identified some internal aspects in Mexico that have shaped the drug business. A factor that is frequently emphasized as one of the main causes of the strength and pervasiveness of illicit groups is the symbiotic relationship between state and criminal organizations (Jones, 2011). Other alleged factors are decentralization, party transitions, and internal economic and social-cultural aspects.

State–Criminal Nexus

The conniving relationship between the state and criminal actors is seen as a key factor in drug cartel empowerment. In Mexico, it is known that drug trafficking is an illicit activity that works from the highest governmental levels. There is another side of this since organized crime can also challenge state authority (Sullivan, 2012). Bailey and Godson (2000), for example, concluded that governability in Mexico could be described as "fragmented contested political-criminal linkages," meaning that the Mexican government has been, for many years, directly defied by organized crime. For instance, the *"plata o plomo"* (silver or lead) threats by the drug cartels oblige governors or political leaders to either work for the organizations or turn a blind eye to their operations, even though they do not want to support them (Grayson, 2014).

Presenting a different perspective, Lupsha and Pimentel (1997) developed a theory that interprets the political–criminal relationship as "elite-exploitative." The model portrays organized crime not as the perpetrators against the state, but instead as "cash cows," manipulated and exploited by government authorities for their own enrichment or with the purpose of financing their political campaigns. According to these authors, Mexico fits this model during the PRI era, but it is not completely strange to present times. This relationship has been shifting throughout time and research has been redirected to investigating the fluctuating dynamics between the state, civil society, and illegal actors.

Nature of the State and Institutional Capacity

The nature of the state and the nature of its institutions are factors that can shape the drug trafficking business. In the work of several authors, the strength of the state, its type of government (e.g., authoritarian, democratic), and weak law enforcement and judiciary institutions are amongst the most important determinants for the establishment and survival capacity of illicit groups (Williams & Godson, 2002; Thoumi, 1995). Thoumi (1995), for example, asserts that low levels of state effectiveness and legitimacy let drug trafficking organizations operate in an environment with a high level of impunity. Following the state weakness argument, Gambetta (1993), when studying the expansion of the Sicilian mafia, found that a weak state maintains conditions under which mafias can easily develop. These groups arise as protectors and providers for the citizenry when the state does not fulfill its role, allowing the mafia to remain deeply rooted in the Italian social, economic and political life (Williams & Godson, 2002).

Not only has the level of strength or weakness of a state been associated with the upsurge of organized crime, but recent literature recognizes that the nature of the government can serve as a breeding place for criminality. Authoritarian regimes with a single-party system are prone to develop strong criminal organizations. This is because there is just a small group of people, or the elite, running the country. There is an absence of checks and balances, which cultivates a weak civil society and reinforces patron–client relations (Williams & Godson, 2002; Shelley, 1999). Shelley (1999) and Ledeneva (2006) posit that the informal networks created during a single-party mandate may lead to the pervasiveness of a strong criminal-political relationship even after a democratic transition. Under this type of regime and governance, the rules of the game for trafficking organizations are established, defined, and maintained by authorities. Once again, Mexico during the PRI era is a good example (Pimentel, 1999). Under this system, political corruption and bribery became strongly entrenched at many levels, from municipal police to high institutional and governmental ranks, in which officials highly benefited from the drug trade. Networks of corruption create a favorable setting for organized crime to operate with impunity (Pimentel, 1999).

Decentralization and Power Party Transitions

Two critical junctures altered the state–criminal relationship in Mexico. One was the decentralization of the federal government during the 1990s, and the second, the end of the PRI regime. Decentralization gave a more accommodating setting for organized crime to develop and become more successful at infiltrating law enforcement institutions at the sub-national level. Cooperative sub-national levels, especially municipal levels, of justice are essential for these groups to succeed (Astorga, 2005; Chabat, 2010; Guerrero-Gutierrez, 2011).

Experts have theorized that party transition is another domestic issue that influences the strength or survival capacity of drug cartels. According to various scholars, changes in incumbent parties weaken a criminal organization's power over a region, affecting its influence and giving an opportunity for other cartels to take over (e.g., Astorga, 2005; Shelley, 1999; Rios, 2013; Dell, 2012; Grayson, 2010). In addition, Trejo and Ley (2012) found that multiparty competition and the democratization of authoritarian regimes affect these organizations' vulnerability.

Santos (2014) disputes the party transition argument. Due to the rapid metastasis of criminal organizations through the Mexican territory during the last ten years, the author contends that there is hardly a relationship between this timing and municipal elections. Nevertheless, the connection is not mutually exclusive. Mexican cartels might be vulnerable to political party shifts; however, they have also shown they quickly adapt to power transitions.

Poverty vs. Rational Choice

Works that attribute domestic economic conditions as an element in the cartels' prevalence are significant in the drug trafficking literature. The drug industry in Mexico is highly profitable, estimates ranging from $8 billion to $25 billion a year (Congressional Research Service, 2013). Coupled with its geographical location next to the single largest marketplace for illegal drugs, the United States, this makes the drug industry for the cartels in Mexico extremely lucrative. As Zill and Bergman (2000) argue, criminal organizations keep operating because they are able to produce drugs at a low cost and sell them to the U.S. at a huge profit margin.[2]

Influenced by the economics field, some scholars focus on the opportunity channels for organized crime that are created in a dysfunctional economy. Economic conditions such as poverty and high unemployment are factors linked to the sizable workforce of the drug trafficking business. According to Rios (2008), the economic benefits of the drug industry are most visible in the employment sector since cartels offer better salaries than many jobs in the formal job market. During the last decade there have been on average close to three million unemployed people in Mexico. In this context, profit from the drug business has been essential to the economy of many municipalities and the source of income for thousands of families (Castañeda, 2009; Zill & Bergman, 2000; Rios, 2008).

The poverty theory has been contended in particular by the rational choice approach. Due to the nature of drug trafficking, the industry employs all sorts, from low skilled workers to highly educated individuals. To put it differently, people do not become drug traffickers because they are poor. There are other aspects that have an important impact such as culture (Adler, 1994). Rational choice evaluates the cost–benefit analysis of joining the cartels. This theory posits that it is not because people are poor or uneducated that they join the drug cartels; instead it is because the gains from working for the illegal industry are greater than the consequences that come with it (e.g., short sentences, or no prosecution at all). This attracts an enormous workforce, and the approximate number of drug employees in Mexico is about 468,000 (Rios, 2008).[3] Mares (2006) argues that this is more likely to happen in places where judicial institutions do not apply the rule of law effectively. Based on rational behavior, criminals exploit market opportunities that come with the demand of illegal or scarce goods and services in order to maximize their profits (Gambetta, 1993; Williams & Godson, 2002).

The Narco Culture

Social acceptability is indispensable for drug cartels to survive. Works that focus on social models emphasize the cultural bases of organized crime and the social mechanisms in which trust and legitimacy are built between organized crime and the communities in which they operate. Intertwined with the political approach, societal explanations also focus on patron–client interactions (Williams & Godson, 2002). In this model, nevertheless, the clientelistic relations are between drug cartels and the citizenry. Cartels provide common goods, invest in infrastructure, offer jobs, or build schools and churches, in exchanges of loyalty and support. Guevara (2013) claims that as the acceptance of the cartels grows, so do their capabilities to recruit, idealize the lifestyle, and naturalize the narco society. In Mexico, the narco culture has been reinforced by *narcocorridos* (folk songs), *narcomantas* (banners), *narcosaints* (religious figures), and *narconovelas* (soap operas), movies, documentaries, and Netflix series (Sullivan, 2012; Guevara, 2013). The narco culture also accentuates a sense of belonging in society, somewhat like the "*la cosa nostra*" motto representative of the Italian mafia.

It is also important to mention that criminal organizations in Mexico resort to forced recruitment as well. Civil and human rights organizations contend that many of the disappearances of civilians in the country relate to this practice. Immigrants from South and Central American countries are targeted by criminal organizations to make them join their ranks for different purposes, from cultivation of the illicit crops, or surveillance, to training them as *sicarios* and for specialized missions (Camacho Servín, 2015).

Criminal Organizations' Characteristics and Structural Topology

Moving from the external and domestic levels of analysis, another strand of works focuses on the actor's attributes (e.g., the criminal organization's structure or *modus operandi*), following a more grassroots approach. Also, in this body of works it is suggested that there is a need to broaden the conceptualization of criminal organizations. The current definition has become unsatisfactory when describing contemporary forms of organized crime, since established characterizations assume more hierarchical structures (Williams & Godson, 2002). This current wave of works suggests that the illicit groups should be denoted instead as "criminal networks."

Departing from Hierarchies

The adoption of social network analysis as an effective and complementary line of research to study the networked structural characteristics of newer forms of criminal organization, has become a growing trend (UN Office of Drug Control, 2010; Sparrow, 1991; Klerks, 2001; Krebs, 2002; Morselli, 2009; Giménez-Salinas, 2011; Bakker et al., 2012; Borgatti, 2006; Bueno de Mesquita & Dickson, 2007; Pereyra, 2012). In this realm of research, it is observed that organizational structures have moved from hierarchies to flatter structures. Experts claim that structural flatness intensifies the resistance of criminal networks in several ways. For example, Kenney (2007) posits that it increases response time; Weick (1976) argues that it decentralizes decision-making allowing for faster restructuration and adaptability. Flatness eases flexibility, as Duijn et al. (2014) put it, and remaining flexible is key to the criminal network's defense against disruption, since these structures are minimally impacted as leadership is removed. This is because they develop mechanisms to insulate central actors of the network, also developing a high degree of redundancy and duplication, which is essential for the groups to continue operations (Williams & Godson, 2002).

In the organizational theory field, authors claim that the survival capacity of an organization is determined by internal structural factors. Braithwaite and Drahos (2000) found that flatness and organizational learning capacity are reciprocal constitutive elements. In other words, in flatter structures information spreads faster, making access to knowledge more homogeneous among its units. This shapes a solid organization in which all its parts are in sync, having access to the same information at the same time.

Arquilla and Ronfeldt (2001) and Kenney (2007) hypothesize that flatter structures make illicit groups more prone to establish strategic alliances with others. For instance, Gower (2008) found that affiliations have proven to make gangs resilient in New Zealand. Adding to this position, some authors have extrapolated the principles from organizational theory to the study of criminal organizations. Garay Salamanca and Salcedo-Albarán (2011), for example, state that networks prefer structural flatness and compartmentalization, as highly compartmentalized cells are most difficult to dismantle, becoming more resistant.

Contrary to the former arguments, other scholars contend that the effect of flat network structures as a strengthening mechanism is sometimes overestimated. Scholars such as Sullivan (2009), Duijn et al. (2014), and Kenney (2007) maintain that compartmentalization might hinder a criminal organization's capacity to survive instead of reinforcing it. They argue that flatness reduces the flow of information among the different parts of the network, depriving it of essential data and intelligence sharing.

Modus Operandi

Finally, seeking to explain the strength or weakness of the Mexican criminal organizations, academics have also focused on their *modus operandi*. Fernandez Menendez and Ronquillo (2006) ascribe the successful expansion of the Zetas to their violent techniques. Nevertheless, Coscia and Rios (2012) dispute such a proposition, arguing that violent tactics alone do not account for the reinforcement and growth of the drug cartel since others are extremely violent as well. Dudley and Rios (2013) maintain that it is the cartel's business strategy which allows them to grow more than other criminal groups. Others, like Osorno (2014), attribute the expansion of the Zetas to their military training background, which has accordingly given them a distinctive competitive advantage.

In a similar vein, Correa-Cabrera and Nava (2011) theorized that it is the "paramilitarization" process of criminal organizations in Mexico that "has become the de facto legitimized purveyor of violence at regional level, effectively supplanting the rule of the State, and placing sociopolitical control in the hands of private individuals" (p. 3). The authors refer to the change in operational and institutional practices by criminal groups, to obtain regional or national supremacy over rival groups and state forces, as the factors that are making them stronger.

Conclusion

Mexico has a long history of drug trafficking. The Mexican cartels have embedded themselves deeply into the government and society, and at high institutional levels. What seems different about the current drug trafficking arena in Mexico and the new cartels is their extremely violent *modus operandi* and the fact that they have diversified their illicit activities. Years before the conflict got out of control, most territories were occupied mainly by a single cartel, and in some cases they shared distribution routes with one another in relative peace. The transition of power from the PRI to the PAN ended the détente between the government and the cartels, ushering in the start of territorial clashes between drug cartels seeking to take over new turf and spreading violence throughout the country.

The militarization of the fight against the cartels has brought negative consequences. One such impact is what authors such as Freeman and Sierra (2005) call the *militarization trap*. This has led to violation of human rights, the abuse of authority, and a lack of coordination among law enforcement bodies. The strategies employed so far have left awful collateral damage in terms of blood and treasure that are not compensate for by the "triumphs" the government has had in detaining kingpins.

Scholars debate whether militarizing the drug war created the recent extreme violence, or if it was avoidable at all. Overall, the reproduction of an imported paradigm has proven unsuccessful. After billions of dollars and years of anti-drug efforts by the U.S. and Mexican governments, the cartels are still operating and some of them do not appear to be slowing down. It seems as if Mexico is experiencing not only a militarization and security trap, but also a "narco trap." Many consider the battling of drug trafficking in Mexico a failed war (Aguilar & Castañeda, 2009; Bailey, 2009).

Notes

1 AMLO is the current president of Mexico. He won the 2018 election running as the presidential candidate of a new political party he established called Movimiento Regeneración Nacional (MORENA).
2 For example, methamphetamines cost approximately $300 to $500 per kilo to produce and are sold in the U.S. for up to $60,000 per kilo. Estimating the profits of this industry is challenging mainly due to the differences in regional prices and in the quality of the products.
3 This figure is equivalent to almost three times the number of employees in PEMEX, the largest state-owned company in Mexico (Rios, 2008).

References

Adler, P. A. (1994). Wheeling and dealing: An ethnography of an upper-level drug dealing and smuggling community. *The Journal of Sociology and Social Welfare*, 21(4), Article 21.
Aguilar, R., & Castañeda, J. (2009). El narco: La guerra fallida. Punto de Lectura.
Althaus, D. (2013). La militarización de México, otra vez. InSight Crime. Retrieved from: http://es.insightcrime.org/analisis/militarizacion-mexico-otra-vez.
Andreas, P. (2003). Redrawing the line. *International Security*, 28(2), 93.
Andreas, P. (2009). *Border games*. Ithaca, NY and London: Cornel University Press.
Andreas, P., & Nadelmann, E. (2006). *Policing the globe: Criminalization and crime control in international relations*. Oxford University Press.
Arquilla, J., & Ronfeldt, D. (2001). *Networks and netwars*. RAND.
Astorga, L. (2004). Mexico: Drugs and politics. In M. Vellinga (Ed.), *The political economy of the drug industry: Latin America and the international system* (pp. 85–102). Gainesville: University of Florida Press.

Astorga, L. (2005). *El siglo de las drogas: El narcotráfico del Porfiriato al nuevo milenio*. Mexico, D.F.: Plaza & Janes.

Astorga, L. (2010). *Drug trafficking organizations and counter-drug strategies in the U.S.–Mexican context*. San Diego: Center for U.S.-Mexican Studies: University of California in San Diego.

Bagley, B. (2005). Globalization and Latin American and Caribbean organized crime. In M. Galeotti, *Global crime today* (pp. 32–53). New York, NY: Routledge.

Bagley, B. (2012). *Drug trafficking and organized crime in the Americas: Major trends in the twenty-first century*. Woodrow Wilson Center.

Bailey, J. (2009). "Security traps" and democratic governability in Latin America. In M. Bergman & L. Whitehead (Eds.), *Criminality, public security, and the challenges of democracy in Latin America*. University of Notre Dame Press.

Bailey, J., & Godson, R. (2000). Introduction. In J. Bailey & R. Godson, *Organized crime and democratic governability: Mexico and the U.S.–Mexican borderlands* (pp. 1–30). Pittsburg, PA: University of Pittsburgh Press.

Bakker, R. M., Raab, J., & Milward, B. (2012). A preliminary theory of dark network resilience. *Journal of Policy Analysis and Management, 31*(1), 33–62.

Borgatti, S. P. (2006). Identifying sets of key players in a social network. *Computer Math Organizational Theory, 12*, 21–34.

Braithwaite, J., & Drahos, P. (2000). *Global business regulation*. Cambridge: Cambridge University Press.

Bueno de Mesquita, E., & Dickson, E. (2007). The propaganda of the deed: Terrorism, counterterrorism, and mobilization. *American Journal of Political Science, 51*(2), 364–381.

Calderón, L., Heinle, K., Rodríguez Ferreira, O., & Shirk, D. A. (2019). *Organized crime and violence in Mexico: Analysis through 2018*. Justice in Mexico. Department of Political Science and International Relations University of San Diego. Retrieved from: https://justiceinmexico.org/wp-content/uploads/2019/04/Organized-Crime-and-Violence-in-Mexico-2019.pdf.

Camacho Servín, F. (2015). Reclutamiento forzoso por el narco, detras de muchos casos de desaparicion: ONG. *La Jornada*. Retrieved from: www.jornada.com.mx/2015/05/03/politica/007n1pol.

Carpenter, T. G. (2003). *Bad neighbor policy*. New York, NY: Palgrave Macmillan.

Carpenter, T. G. (2012). *The fire next door: Mexico's drug violence and the danger to America*. Washington, DC: Cato Institute.

Carreño de la Rosa, F. (2011). Para que la droga no llegue a tus hijos. SDPnoticias. Retrieved from: www.sdpnoticias.com/columnas/2011/02/28/para-que-la-droga-no-llegue-a-tus-hijos.

Carvajal-Dávila, R. (1998). *Todo lo que Usted deberia saber sobre el crimen organizado en Mexico*. Mexico: Oceano.

Castañeda, R. A. (2009). *El narco: La guerra fallida de Mexico*. Mexico: Punto de Lectura.

Chabat, J. (2010). *Combatting drugs in Mexico under Calderon: The inevitable war*. CIDE No. 205.

Congressional Research Service. (2013). *2013 annual report of the Congressional Research Service*. Retrieved from: www.scribd.com/doc/296990679/2013-Annual-Report-of-the-Congressional-Research-Service.

Correa-Cabrera, G., & Nava, J. (2011). *Drug wars, social networks and the right to information: The rise of informal media as the freedom of press's lifeline in northern Mexico*. APSA 2011 Annual Meeting Paper.

Coscia, M., & Rios, V. (2012). *Knowing where and how criminal organizations operate using web content*. Maui, HI: CIKM'12.

Cutrona, S. (2017). *Challenging the U.S.-led war on drugs: Argentina in comparative perspective*. New York, NY: Routledge.

Dell, M. (2012). *Trafficking networks and the Mexican drug war*. Harvard.

Dudley, S., & Rios, V. (2013). Why Mexico's Zetas expanded faster than their rivals. InSight Crime. Aug 14. Retrieved from: www.insightcrime.org/news/analysis/why-mexicos-zetas-expanded-faster-rivals/.

Duijn, P. A., Kashirin, V., & Sloot, P. M. (2014). The relative ineffectiveness of criminal network disruption. *Scientific Reports, 4*, 4238.

Duran-Martinez, A. (2018). *The politics of drug violence: Criminals, cops, and politicians in Colombia and Mexico*. Oxford University Press.

Eiss, P. K. (2014). The narcomedia. *Latin American Perspectives, 41*(2; Issue 195), 78–98.

Fernandez Menedez, J., & Ronquillo, V. (2006). *De los mars a los zetas los secretos del narcotrafico, de Colombia a Chicago*. Editorial Grijalbo.

Franco, M. (2018). El caso Ayotzinapa: Cuatro años de dolor e incentidumbre. *New York Times, America Latina*, September 26 2018. Retrieved from: www.nytimes.com/es/2018/09/26/espanol/america-latina/ayotzinapa-estudiantes-43-mexico.html.

Freeman, J., & Sierra, J. L. (2005). *Mexico: The militarization trap*. In C. Youngers and E. Rosin (Eds.), *Drugs and democracy in Latin America* (pp. 263–302). Boulder, CO: Lynne Rienner.

Fregoso, J. (2017). Pueblos fantasma: El saldo invisible de la guerra narco en Mexico. Infobae Mexico. Retrieved from: www.infobae.com/america/mexico/2017/07/02/pueblos-fantasma-el-saldo-invisible-de-la-guerra-narco-en-mexico/.

Gambetta, D. (1993). *The Sicilian Mafia*. Cambridge, MA: Harvard University Press.

Garay Salamanca, L. J., and Salcedo-Albarán, E. (2011). *Drug trafficking corruption and states: How illicit networks reconfigure institutions in Colombia, Guatemala and Mexico*. Bogotá, Colombia: Fundación Método.

Giménez-Salinas, A. (2011). Illegal networks or criminal organizations. Archives Ceruim. Retrieved from http://archives.cerium.ca/IMG/pdf/Gimenez_Salinas_Framis_-_Illegal_Networks_Or_Criminal_Organizations.pdf.

Gobierno de Mexico. (2019). *Estrategia nacional de seguridad publica*. Retrieved from: www.gob.mx/cms/uploads/attachment/file/434517/Estrategia_Seguridad-ilovepdf-compressed-ilovepdf-compressed-ilovepdf-compressed__1_.pdf.

Gootenberg, P. (2011). Cocaine's blowback north: A pre-history of Mexican drug violence. *LASA Forum, 42*(2), 7–10.

Gower, P. (2008). Gang presence growing since early days in Otara. *New Zealand Herald*.

Grayson, G. W. (2010). *Mexico: Narco-violence and a failed state?* New Brunswick and London: Transaction Publishers.

Grayson, G. W. (2014). *The cartels: The story of Mexico's most dangerous criminal organizations and their impact on U.S. security*. Santa Barbara, CA: Praeger.

Grillo, I. (2011). *El narco: Inside Mexico's criminal insurgency*. New York, NY: Bloomsbury Press.

Guerrero-Gutierrez, E. (2011). *Security, drugs, and violence in Mexico: A survey.* Washington, DC: 7th North American Forum.
Guevara, A. Y. (2013). Propaganda in Mexico's drug war. *Journal of Strategic Security,* 6(3, suppl.), 131–151.
Isacson, A. (2005). The U.S. military in the war on drugs. In C. Youngers & E. Rosin (Eds.), *Drugs and democracy in Latin America* (pp. 263–302). Boulder, CO: Lynne Rienner.
Jones, N. P. (2011). *The state reaction: A theory of illicit network resilience.* Irvine: University of California.
Kassab, H., & Rosen, J. (2019). *Corruption, institutions, and fragile states.* Palgrave.
Kenney, M. (2007). *From Pablo to Osama: Trafficking and terrorist networks.* Pennsylvania State University Press.
Klerks, P. (2001). The network paradigm applied to criminal organizations: Theoretical nitpicking or a relevant doctrine for investigators? Recent developments in the Netherlands. *Connections,* 24(3), 53–65.
Krebs, V. E. (2002). Mapping networks of terrorist cells. *Connections,* 24(3), 43–52.
Ledeneva, A. (2006). *How Russia really works.* Ithaca, NY: Cornell University.
Loveman, B. (2006). U.S. security policies in Latin America and the Andean region, 1990–2006. In B. Loveman (Ed.), *Addicted to failure: U.S. security policy in Latin America and the Andean region* (pp. 1–52). Boulder, CO: Rowman and Littlefield.
Lupsha, P. A., & Pimentel, S. A. (1997). The nexus between crime and politics: Mexico. *Trends in Organized Crime,* 3(1), 65–67.
Mares, D. R. (2006). *Drug wars and coffeehouses: The political economy of the international drug trade.* Washington, DC: CQ Press.
McKibben, C. (2015). NAFTA and drug trafficking: Perpetuating violence and the illicit supply chain. March 20. Council on Hemispheric Affairs. Retrieved from: www.coha.org/nafta-and-drug-trafficking-perpetuating-violence-and-the-illicit-supply-chain/.
Melesio, L. (2019). Case of 43 Ayotzinapa missing students unresolved five years on. Aljazeera, September 26. Retrieved from: www.aljazeera.com/indepth/features/case-43-ayotzinapa-missing-students-unresolved-years-190926204902655.html.
Morselli, C. (2009). *Inside criminal networks.* Montreal: Springer.
Office of the United States Trade Representative. (2019). *Mexico: U.S.–Mexico trade facts.* Retrieved from: https://ustr.gov/countries-regions/americas/mexico.
Osorno, D. E. (2014). How a Mexican cartel demolished a town, incinerated hundreds of victims, and got away with it. VICE News Mexico. Retrieved from: https://news.vice.com/article/how-a-mexican-cartel-demolished-a-town-incinerated-hundreds-of-victims-and-got-away-with-it.
Pereyra, G. (2012). México: Violencia criminal y "guerra contra el narcotráfico." *Revista Mexicana de Sociología,* 74, 429–460.
Pimentel, S. A. (1999). Nexus of organized crime and politics in Mexico: Mexico's legacy of corruption. *Trends in Organized Crime,* 4(3), 9–28.
Ramos, J. (2013). El México de Peña Nieto: Mas violencia, pocos resultados. Opinion. Retrieved from: http://opinion.infobae.com/jorge-ramos/2013/12/04/el-mexico-de-pena-nieto-mas-violencia-pocos-resultados/.
Resendiz, F. (2006). Rinde AMLO protesta como presidente legitimo. *El Universal.* Retrieved from: http://archivo.eluniversal.com.mx/notas/389114.html.
Rios, V. (2008). Evaluating the economic impact of drug traffic in Mexico. Unpublished working paper.

Rios, V. (2012). *How government structure encourages criminal violence: The causes of Mexico's drug war.* Cambridge, MA: Harvard University.

Rios, V. (2013). Why did Mexico become so violent? A self-reinforcing violent equilibrium caused by competition and enforcement. *Trends in Organized Crime, 16*(2), 138–155.

Santos, Y. (2014). La metástasis del crimen organizado en México. ABC Mundo. Retrieved from: www.abc.es/internacional.20141024/abci-mexico-crimen-organizado-2014102318.

Schendel, W., & Abraham, I. (Eds.). (2005). *Illicit flows and criminal things: States, borders, and the other side of globalization.* Indiana University Press.

Shelley, L. (1999). *Identifying, counting and categorizing transnational criminal organizations.* National Criminal Justice Reference Service, 1–18.

Snyder, R., & Duran-Martinez, A. (2009). Drugs, violence, and state-sponsored protection rackets in Mexico and Colombia. *Colombia Inter nacional*, (70), 61–91. Retrieved from: www.scielo.org.co/scielo.php?script=sci_arttext&pid=S0121-56122009000200004&lng=en&tlng=en.

Sparrow, M. K. (1991). The application of network analysis to criminal intelligence: An assessment of the prospects. *Social Networks, 13*, 251–274.

Sullivan, A. (2009). The Revolution will be Twittered. *The Atlantic.*

Sullivan, J. P. (2012). *From drug wars to criminal insurgency: Mexican cartels, criminal enclaves and criminal insurgency in Mexico and Central America: Implications for Global Security.* FMSH Working Paper 9, FMSH-WP-2012-09. Paris: Fondation Maison des sciences de l'homme.

Sullivan, J. P., & Bunker, R. J. (2011). Rethinking insurgency: criminality, spirituality, and societal warfare in the Americas. *Small Wars & Insurgencies, 22*(5), 742–763

Thoumi, F. (1995). *Political economy and illegal drugs in Colombia.* London: Lynne Rienner.

Tokatlian, J., & Bagley, B. (2007). *Economía y política del narcotráfico.* Universidad de los Andes.

Trejo, G., & Ley, S. (2012). *Votes, drugs, and violence: Subnational democratization and the onset of inter-cartel wars in Mexico 1995–2006.* University of Notre Dame.

United Nations Office on Drugs and Crime. (2010). *World drug report.* New York, NY: United Nations.

United Nations Office on Drugs and Crime. (2017). *World drug report: Executive summary, conclusions, and policy implications.* Retrieved from: www.unodc.org/wdr2017/field/Booklet_1_EXSUM.pdf.

Valdés Castellanos, G. (2013). *Historia del narcotrafico en Mexico.* Mexico: Aguilar.

Weick, K. (1976). Education systems as loosely coupled systems. *Administrative Science Quarterly, 21*, 1–19.

Williams, P. (2009). Illicit markets, weak states and violence: Iraq and Mexico. *Crime, Law and Social Change, 52*, 323–336.

Williams, P., & Godson, R. (2002). Anticipating organized and transnational crime. *Crime, Law and Social Change, 37*(4), 311–355.

Youngers, C., & Rosin, E. (Eds.). (2005). *Drugs and democracy in Latin America: The impact of U.S. policy.* Boulder, CO: Lynne Rienner.

Zill, O., & Bergman, L. (2000). U.S. business and money laundering. Frontline. PBS online. Retrieved from: www.pbs.org/wgbh/pages/frontline/shows/drugs/special/us.html.

Chapter 2

Social Media
The Continuation of War by Other Means

The media has played a central role in the Mexican fight against drugs; as in other conflicts, it has been used as a powerful instrument for war. During World War II, the Nazis used the media as a propaganda weapon to antagonize the Jews and legitimize a heinous program of ethnic cleansing. In the U.S., during both world wars, the media was used as a tool for recruiting American soldiers, best captured in the famous campaign portraying Uncle Sam with the historical slogan "I want you." The antagonistic propaganda between the U.S. and the U.S.S.R. during the Cold War is another example of the major influence of media during warfare. Lately, terrorist groups such as Al Qaeda and ISIS have also used media, mainly social media, to fight their wars, with similar goals. They have used the web-based platforms as public relations instruments, to win people's "hearts and minds," and to antagonize Western ideologies, to legitimate violence and to gain supporters.

In academia, the perception of social media as a communication tool started with a positive and hopeful view. From its beginnings, scholarly works portrayed these new communication platforms as a tool for the masses to organize and communicate their political concerns. It was predicted that social media platforms would become important agents of change from below, providing an outlet for exposure, usually reserved for selective groups, with the potential of providing a mechanism to deepen political accountability and democracy (Howard, et al., 2011; Müller & Hübner, 2014). These works developed principally after several powerful mass demonstrations around the world arose during the first decade of the twenty-first century, such as the Arab Spring and protests in Tunisia and Moldova (Morozov, 2009). Empirical evidence suggests that the so-called "Twitter revolutions" were successful at overturning long-standing authoritarian establishments such as the Mubarak regime in Egypt (Sullivan, 2009). The aftermath of some of the revolutions might not have included the desired political change, yet they highlighted the utilization of social media as an influential tool for grassroots mass organization playing a key role in historic social movements. It is important to emphasize that social media worked as an intervening variable, rather than a causal one, when studying the causes of the Arab Spring revolutions (Drezner & Farrell, 2004; Segerberg & Bennett, 2011). Howard et al. (2011) found that Facebook functioned as a central node in networks of political dissent in Egypt, concluding that: "[s]ocial media alone did not cause political upheaval in North Africa. But information technologies ... altered the capacity of citizens and civil society actors to affect domestic politics" (p. 23). The early euphoria of these events raised important questions on the impact of social media in politics.

As the wave of social movements was peaking in the Middle East, in Mexico, social media was also having a social impact. The utilization of new media in Mexico, however, rather than being as a successful tool for civilians to organize protests against the upsurge of violence and impunity reigning over the country, has been somewhat different. On the one hand, social media has been useful for citizens in Mexico, living in the most affected areas, as a major source of information about shootings, or blockades. On the other hand, it has also been highly beneficial for drug cartels, helping to advance their criminal strategies.

This chapter explores the role of the media in the Mexican drug war and the transition between the usage of traditional media and the adoption of web-based platforms as main sources of information, changing the dynamics of the conflict and its mechanisms of control. First, the chapter analyzes the social media paradox and the theoretical contributions put forward in the literature about the benefits (i.e., power) and challenges (i.e., vulnerability) the adoption of social media might bring to criminal organizations. Second, it presents an overview of how the media has been instrumental to the government, the drug cartels, and the citizenry, pursuing different purposes and agendas during the Mexican war on drugs. In addition, it offers a brief account of the methodological and theoretical grounds of social network analysis, highlighting its relevance to advance research into criminal behavior on social media.

Criminal Organizations on Social Media: The Social Media Paradox

In the social and political sciences, studies on social media became particularly focused on topics related to transnational social movements, government accountability, political unrest, and public opinion, among others. Soon after, research shifted towards the study of terrorists groups, such as Al Qaeda and later ISIS, grabbing academic attention after utilizing social media to expose their crusade of terror. It was during the summer of 2014 when the beheading of the American journalist James Foley was broadcasted by the terrorist organization via YouTube. The message targeted the U.S., to express the group's resentment and hatred towards the nation for its historical involvement in the Middle East. The impressive spread and worldwide attention that gravitated towards ISIS after the cruel act gave birth to a social media model tainted with blood.

After this, discussion revolved around understanding the purposes for which terrorist groups or criminal organizations were choosing to adopt social media in their strategies and whether these online platforms could strengthen or weaken them. Research has attempted to explain the phenomenon, focusing on three main factors: (i) social media as an enabler of structural flatness; (ii) social media as a force multiplier; and (iii) social media as a tool for psychological warfare.

As previously mentioned, pioneer studies on social media focus on the way civilians have used it to organize and communicate their political views. The news of the demonstrations in Egypt went viral and the entire world witnessed the revolution, which also spread to other countries in Northern Africa. The impetus the communication platforms gave to these social movements raised important political issues and broadened the conversation regarding the spread of democracy to more countries in the world or the shift of power and control between governments and civil society. As history unfolds, nevertheless, the view of social media and the promising prospects it seemed to offer have been obscured by the realities the world is facing today. Besides the inability of some Arab countries to reestablish politically, of particular concern has been the rise of extreme fundamentalist terrorist groups such as ISIS, or ISIL, that found in social media an effective tool of exposure. Paradoxically, the same instrument that helped bring nations to freedom is the same one extremists have used to terrorize the world.

With the arising of the latter concern, a change in the literature is perceivable. A second wave of works with a less hopeful and more skeptical view of social media emerged, focusing largely on its usage by terrorist organizations. Yet, ISIS is not the only criminal group to use social media. In Mexico, the utilization of the web-based outlets took a dark turn as well. From working as a platform to fill the informational vacuum and as a means for survival and protection of citizens, it became an instrument used by the drug cartels for warfare strategies.

In Mexico, both the government and the drug cartels have adopted media outlets to enhance their tactics during the war on drugs. In this case, its utilization turned out to be somehow atypical. In other words, the use of social media by the actors involved in the conflict goes beyond recruiting and legitimation practices. During the Mexican war on drugs, the media regarded as reliable transitioned from traditional or mainstream forms (TV, radio), to new alternative web-based platforms (Facebook, Twitter, YouTube). In this context, the utilization of new media thrived and these platforms started to become the medium through which citizens got information and reported about the war. Soon, drug cartels realized the potential benefits of the open source communication outlets and rapidly established their presence in cyberspace. This transformed in a way the landscape of the conflict and the dynamics among actors. Social media in Mexico dramatically changed the way the drug war has been reported and "followed" ever since.

Social Network Analysis

Significant contributions to the field of social network analysis (SNA) can be traced back to the 1960s and 1970s, accomplished by sociologists such as Granovetter (1973) furthering our understanding of theory and method. Years earlier (1940 to mid-1950s), the work of social anthropologists such as Siegried Nadel and Alfred Radcliffe-Brown influenced forthcoming research, presenting ideas about the connection between social patterns and structures. The rise of a "networked society" has sparked and attracted a significant amount of research on online social networks around the world (Castells, 2000). Other important inputs were developed by social psychologist Stanley Milgram whose *six degrees of separation* popularized the small-world idea, arguing that everyone is linked to everybody else through a few highly connected intermediaries (Knoke & Yang, 2008). More recently, a higher appeal to network analysis came with technological internet-based online social networks or social media with the proliferation of sites such as Facebook and Twitter. The network perspective has provided new opportunities to reinstate standard social and behavioral science research questions by rethinking networked interactions in political, economic, or social contexts (Wasserman & Faust, 1994).

Structural characteristics of social networks have been broadly studied to better understand and explain human interaction and behavior within networks (Freeman, 2004; Shapiro & Varian, 1999). In the social sciences, it is widely assumed that actors make decisions and act independently of the behavior or influence of other actors. Whether analyzed as utility-maximizing rational calculations, or motivation-based actions, the explanations mainly consider the individual attributes, setting aside the broader interaction contexts within which social actors are embedded (Knoke & Yang, 2008). In contrast, network analysis assumes that actors participate and exist within social systems that connect them to other actors, and that these relations influence their behavior, which brings valuable insights in understanding the dynamics of criminal organizations.

There is extensive literature dedicated to the study of criminal organizations and intelligence using social network analysis as a method to identify and visualize, through graphs, social relationships and group dynamics among actors (Garay Salamanca & Salcedo-Albarán, 2011; Sparrow, 1991). In the criminology field, social network analyses have been implemented to identify structural features of illicit networks (Morselli, 2009), to look at criminal networks resilience (Jones, 2016) and criminal networks disruption (Duijn et al., 2014), to trace networks of corruption

(Garay Salamanca & Salcedo-Albarán, 2011), and to predict behavior (Renfro & Deckro, 2001; Aftergood, 2004; Koschade, 2006).

Some other works have been dedicated to terrorist organizations (Arquilla & Ronfeldt, 2001; Krebs, 2002). Krebs (2002) presented the most insightful social network analysis of a terrorist organization. He examined the network of Al Qaeda after the September 11 attacks. The significance of his findings is to demonstrate that social network analysis is a valuable tool for law enforcement and the intelligence community to advance their understanding of criminal organizations (Koschade, 2006). The next section explores the structural opportunities the utilization of social media can provide to criminal groups.

Flatter Structures and Social Media

Drawing from SNA, scholars have attempted to examine the effects of technology and social media on criminal or dark networks. There is a certain consensus about the idea that with the adoption of technology, criminal organizations have left aside rigid hierarchical structures, adopting instead flatter, more flexible, innovative, and decentralized, often cell-like, configurations (Arquilla & Ronfeldt, 2001; Kenney, 2007; Pereyra, 2012; Wagley, 2006; Giménez-Salinas, 2011; McAdam, Tarrow, & Tilly, 2001). As Arquilla and Ronfeldt (2001: p. 5) put it:

> [T]oday, the key form of organization on the rise is the network, ... [the] new information technologies render the ability to connect and coordinate the actions of widely distributed 'nodes' in almost unprecedented ways. Whoever masters this form will accrue advantages of a substantial nature.

The reasoning behind this idea is that the adoption of the social web-based platforms permits the organization to operate in a more decentralized manner. Conversely, other authors suggest that criminal organizations' exposure to these technological channels does not give the organizations more power; rather, it can increase the risk of attacks that can result in their demise, whether they are hierarchical or not (Duijn et al., 2014).

Social Media as a Force Multiplier

Another strand of relevant theorizing argues that the utilization of social media platforms may lead to the strengthening of a criminal organization due to the conjecture that these outlets offer opportunities to reach potential new members, to recruit and radicalize, and to legitimize organizations' actions. In a report published by the London-based International Centre for the Study of Radicalization (2014), researchers tracked the extent to which ISIS could attract foreign fighters through social media. For a period of 12 months, analysts examined more than 18,000 Twitter accounts and found that some users served as "disseminators," individuals who are highly influential and effective in recruiting foreign fighters. Thanks to social media platforms, disseminators can be based anywhere in the world, targeting wider audiences and making them hard to track. Similarly, Rothkopf (2015) recognizes that social media has served as an effective force multiplier to spread ISIS's ideologies. The author contends that the latter is a leap forward from the hierarchically structured, closed club-like terrorist organizations like Al Qaeda or guerrilla groups such as the FARC.

Stern and Berger (2015) conducted a study exploring the personal Twitter accounts of various ISIS members. Through content analysis, they found that the terrorist group use their accounts to "brag about military victories, harass their enemies, and rally supporters from their respective regions and around the world" (p. 135). These authors recognize that social media has opened the door to alternative types of interactions and has reinforced connectivity, which has contributed to the strengthening of the organization. Following the same line of thought, Duijn et al. (2014) propose that a criminal organization's exposure on social media channels intensifies its chances of increasing its lines of support since these platforms facilitate contact and access to followers' information, as well as attracting more people.

Similarly, Gilsinan (2015) argues that in some cases it is easier for these groups to gain followers online, especially when they find and reach an audience already radicalized. Aday et al. (2010) found that the new media encourages self-segregation and polarization, especially in young minds. People usually seek online information that reinforces their beliefs, and this offers an opportunity for the criminal organization to induce hatred.

Studies have argued that by monitoring ISIS members' and supporters' activities on social media, indicators of future behavior can be depicted. Johnson et al. (2016) examined longitudinal records of ISIS online activity on Facebook. In this study, the authors developed a statistical model aimed at identifying behavioral patterns among online supporters. The study finds that with this information it is possible to predict early stages in the planning of a major violent event. The results of the research propose that the increase of connectivity through the online platforms can facilitate the formation of physical organized groups to plan attacks.

Other important research claims that online participation is not as strong as is commonly believed. These studies find that online participation has become a substitute for real action. For instance, many online ISIS supporters engage just virtually, avoiding exposing themselves to the risks of field activities (Berger & Morgan, 2015). Additionally, Berger and Morgan (2015), and Jones (2016) hypothesize that online networks are not strong, since they produce only "weak ties." In other words, the support followers offer online does not necessarily translate into the physical world. In fact, some authors present evidence suggesting that social media content in general tends to discourage extremist behavior in the wider population.

Social Media as Tool for Psychological Warfare

Even though social media platforms have allowed criminal organizations to distribute powerful messages and sensitive images, experts consider that such approaches can work as a double-edged sword also known as the "social media paradox" (Farwell, 2014; Rothkopf, 2015). Security experts have stated that ISIS success on social media has helped them keep a high number of members and recruits. On the one hand, these groups show their "good side." For example, ISIS posts pictures and videos of soldiers playing with kittens. Similarly, drug cartels in Mexico, such as the Gulf cartel, uploaded videos on YouTube broadcasting images of members distributing food and clothes for the victims of hurricane Ingrid that devastated the coasts of Tamaulipas and Veracruz in 2013. On the other hand, these groups also post gruesome videos of beheadings, tortures, or rapes to intimidate their enemies and instigate fear in the population. Experts suggests that these types of messages that criminal groups distribute in cyberspace can either be successful at convincing people they are "the good guys," or can also be held against them (Farwell, 2014; Dale, 2014). In the following chapters, this book presents three case studies on different Mexican drug cartels and it attempts to analyze their online behavior, the main reasons why they use social media, and whether the utilization of these platforms has empowered them, or, to the contrary, made them more vulnerable. The next section presents a brief account of the role of social media in the Mexican drug war.

Social Media in the Mexican Drug War

In Mexico, the study of social media also turned into a subject of interest among researchers when its usage exploded in the country by the end of 2010. These works largely focus on the use of social media by civilians, with a few on the use of internet-based platforms by organized crime. Many analyses dedicated to Mexican drug cartels on social media are limited to journalistic accounts, but just a few present rigorous methodologies.

Monroy-Hernandez, boyd, Kiciman, De Choudhury, and Counts (2013) conducted a study monitoring the use of social media as participatory news platforms by people living in armed-conflict environments. Combining content and quantitative Twitter data exploration, the authors present a descriptive analysis of the general participation patterns of ordinary citizens. They collected data for a 16-month period (August 2010–November 2011), in four Mexican cities: Monterrey, Reynosa, Saltillo, and Veracruz. The results indicate that a sizable number of tweets were reports of violent events that included a specific location. The outcomes also show the rise of citizens as information wardens. This indicates that existing media apparatuses were not meeting the public need. The authors conclude that the rise of social media as an alternative information channel has enabled the emergence of civic media curators. The terms "media curator" or "information curator" refer to the people or accounts that receive, respond to, or retweet dozens of posts from other accounts to disseminate information (Monroy-Hernandez et al., 2013).

Coscia and Rios (2012) constructed a model using Google's search engine to trace the behavior of cartels' mobility and *modus operandi*. Developing a computerized search algorithm, they found that some Mexican drug cartels, during the drug war years, became more aggressive, expansionist, and competitive. Their results also suggest that cartels are open to exposing themselves online, noting that there is a considerable volume of information about these groups floating around cyberspace.

Social media became another battleground for conflict between drug cartels, government, civilians and self-defense groups (e.g., Eiss, 2014; Monroy-Hernandez et al., 2013; Correa-Cabrera & Nava, 2011). Kan (2013) followed and analyzed the case of an online clash that took place during the fall of 2011 between the Zetas and the international hacker group Anonymous. The drug cartel kidnapped several members of Anonymous during a demonstration in the coastal state of Veracruz. In response, Anonymous threatened the Zetas via a YouTube video giving an ultimatum to the cartel to free their peers; otherwise, they would publicly reveal and expose the cartel's entire operating network (from taxi drivers to top politicians). Kan states that even though both actors used the virtual domain to fight what he called a "cyberwar of the underworld," the incident had public consequences that left the Mexican government as a spectator in the conflict. He proposes that this confrontation revealed that criminal organizations are vulnerable to cyberattacks. The study concludes that the release of the Anonymous members demonstrates that this form of coercion via cyberspace can be effective at targeting criminal organizations like the Zetas.

Recent work has attempted to provide deeper methodical analysis of the Mexican cartels in social media with the utilization of social network analysis. Nix, Smith, Petrocelli, and Rojek (2016) presented a study that examines the way self-proclaimed cartel members utilize social media to further their criminal activities. Employing an open-coding, qualitative analysis strategy, the study surveyed the content of 75 accounts for a period of four months. They found individual accounts posting evidence of being part of the criminal hierarchy, self-admission, and evidence of criminal activity. The second part of their study implemented social network analysis to explore the relationships among the 75 accounts investigated. The SNA underlines the individuals' cartel affiliations, as well as the relationships among cartels, which aligns with the general narrative of what we know about them. For example, it reflects the association of the Zetas with the Gulf cartel as well as the affiliation of the group Antrax with the Sinaloa cartel. Some of the outcomes presented in the study resonate with the findings presented in this book, which takes a more systematic approach.

Media Censorship and the Adoption of Social Media

From the beginning of the Mexican conflict, traditional media (TV, radio, journals) played a key role serving as a tool for the government and the cartels to spread their respective messages. As noted previously, the media was strategically used by Calderón's cabinet to construct an image in which the government justified the militarization of the war on drugs. To promote the new drug policy, the government used printed media, radio, and TV spots, showing images of successful operations and the capture of capos or cartel members. The images became familiar; they consistently showed the military in their uniforms holding high-caliber weapons, criminals by their side handcuffed and looking down as a gesture of shame and surrender. Sometimes the broadcasted images presented confiscated drugs, money, guns, and ammunition, all laid out in front of the captured cartel members. These images flooded the media during the first years of Calderón's militarized approach, with the aim of convincing citizens of its "effectiveness" and "essentiality."

Freedom of speech and freedom of the press is not a right that has been particularly embraced in Mexico. The World Press Freedom Index (2018) ranked the country at 144, out of 180 countries, suggesting that the state and powerful communication conglomerates significantly control the information available to the public. Mexico's media system is unique and it does not exactly fit traditional models (Hallin, 2000). For example, the Mexican media does not fulfill the "watchdog" function that characterizes other Western media in which the press is employed as a mechanism for "checks and balances" and government accountability (Waisbord, 1996). Nor does it obey the partisan model in which the press exposes diverse points of view. Rather, mass media in Mexico has been an important part of the political power structure used by the government as an "ideological state apparatus" (Hallin, 2000). There is privatization of media in the country, but it has a tight relationship with the state (Adler, 1993; Hallin, 2000).

Mexico is home to one of the major television conglomerates in Latin America and holds a sizable market share in the U.S. *Televisa* has for many years controlled much of the news and stories that are reported throughout the nation. Until recently, *Televisa*'s news division was the main producer of broadcast news and it has been a key player during presidential elections (Hallin, 2000). Images of candidates' gatherings or campaign meetings have been edited and manipulated to favor or disfavor a particular political party in exchange for great sums of money (Adler, 1993). *Televisa* shows control over the media by, for example, vetoing journalists for publishing scandals or negative notes that compromise the government's reputation. A contemporary case was the dismissal of news anchor Carmen Aristegui after she reported on the "white house" scandal that involved the First Lady at the time Angelica Rivera, investors, and government officials. Given the expedient relationship between the media and the government, other contemporary sources of information have been created. One of the first of a series of news publications, which has established a more independent form of media, is the weekly magazine *Proceso* or ZETA in Tijuana (Hallin, 2000). These magazines served as one of the principal sources of information during the drug war along with other forms of alternative press, discussed below.

For their part, drug cartels have also used media as a war instrument. The media has helped cartels boost the popularity of the "narco culture" (Estrin, 2011; Cockrell, 2011). In some parts of the country, drug lords have become epic heroes, even saints, like Jesús Malverde, a figure whom cartel members venerate and pray to for protection. The narco lifestyle has become desirable, especially among younger generations that grew up during the war years, and have been exposed all their lives to the popular *narcocorridos*, *narconovelas*, movies, and TV series. The media has glorified and demonized them, but, as the saying goes, there is no such thing as bad publicity.

Cartels in Mexico take advantage of media exposure. They also control communication outlets in certain areas. Local TV stations' or newspapers' headquarters have closed their doors after being bombed or threatened, or have had their journalists killed by criminal organizations (Lara, 2012). To avoid giving the cartels a free ride as regards media exposure, in 2011, 50 major news outlets and 665 other Mexican broadcasting organizations signed an agreement proposed by the government. The pact sought to prevent the press from becoming an instrument for criminal organizations to spread their messages and terror (Medel, 2011). After that, the flow of information regarding the war on drugs decreased significantly; only a few scattered reports about the war were available in the national and local news.

As a result, the cartels started to improvise their own news bulletins and broaden their channels of publicity to get the media's attention, by throwing human heads in public plazas and in front of government buildings, for example. Another method was the use of *narcomantas*, messages written on blankets hanging off overpasses, which mostly target rival cartels or government officials. Eventually, the criminal groups started to adopt the internet to spread their messages, creating websites, Facebook and Twitter pages, and posting gruesome videos on YouTube of real beheadings, killings, and torture of members of rival cartels.

A key incident that marked the beginning of the "new normal" in Mexico happened in the northern border area, when citizens started reporting on social media the remnants of shootings and turf disputes between rival cartels. In February 2010, former governor of the state of Tamaulipas Eugenio Hernandez declared: "There is nothing going on in the northern part of the state [Tamaulipas]," and when questioned by the press with regards to the sudden wave of violence that struck the area at that time, "the citizens are being psychotic," he affirmed (Daño Colateral, 2010: p. 1). In the news, no reports. The nature of the wave of violence experienced by citizens in the border towns was so brutal and shocking that statements like those from former governor Hernandez and other officials, ignoring and hiding the severity of the situation, roused the indignation and resentment of the population. To refute the official discourse, outraged civilians began to post videos and images of the violence on social media. The rest of the country and the world started to have access to the truth about the shootings and devastation of war zones in the north, highly denied by the government. Unidentified citizens of Ciudad Camargo, Tamaulipas, posted some of the first videos originating from the frontlines of the drug war on YouTube and they went viral. This city became a war zone overnight, when the Zetas parted from the Gulf cartel and started fighting over important traffic and transport points between Tamaulipas and Texas.

It became evident to civilians that the media had been silenced and controlled by the government, or the drug cartels. It is not surprising that sometimes news involving organized crime reached the Mexican public through reports from the neighboring country. In the towns along the frontier, news about shootings or violent confrontations is often reported in the U.S. media, while in Mexico there are no reports.

In this context, the perceived reliability of traditional news sources fell significantly. From this point on, social media became the routine source for reports and information about violent confrontations between cartels and the military, rival groups, and street blockades. Social media emerged as a medium to cover the drug war in response to the informational vacuum left by traditional media outlets. Many Mexicans living in the most violent cities found on these web-based platforms tools for "information and survival" (Cave, 2011). Residents often go to Twitter to see if there has been a shooting on their route to work or on their way to their children's school.

The New "Face" of the Drug War

The signing of the censorship of the media agreement in 2011 and the spike of social media usage marks a critical point in the development of the drug conflict. In some ways, the dynamics of the drug war and the interactions among actors altered. Social media outlets became crucial portals through which the players in the war and those affected by it follow different agendas. Control over the information on social media, decentralized and complex in nature, grew into yet another space for the government and the cartels to continue their fight.

Twitter, Facebook, and YouTube developed into the principal internet-based sites that have become part of the everyday life of approximately 28 million Mexicans. In 2011, Facebook saw a spike in its use in the country with a 154 percent increase compared to the previous year (Reuters, 2011). This same year, three of the most popular blogs in Mexico, *Blog del Narco*, *Mil Cincuenta*, and *Frontera al Rojo Vivo*, were created to report on the narco-violence, rapidly becoming favorites among the citizens. After a couple of months, *Blog del Narco* averaged a traffic of three million visits per week (*La Nación*, 2010).

This study suggests that the transition from traditional to social media allowed for the dynamics of the drug war to change, adding civilians as active participants in the conflict. There are several cases that illustrate the inclusion of citizens in the war. A case in point is the already mentioned incident referred as the "cyber war" between the hacktivist group Anonymous and the Zetas. Another case is the near real-time posting of the assassination of Dr. Maria del Rosario Fuentes Rubio. An additional case that appears to be the first documented murder related to social media users and bloggers, according to the Committee to Protect Journalists (CPJ), was the case of Maria Elizabeth Macías who reported on the cartels using the pseudonym "NenaDLaredo." Interestingly, the reporting from civilians about the drug war-related happenings was evidently greater in areas where the Zetas operate. This is further discussed in Chapter 4.

In addition, to end the oppression of mainstream media communication channels, the purpose of the emergent civilian-journalism and cyber activism was for people to have truthful information on the war instead of the fragmented version delivered by the government. A resident of the state of Tamaulipas, who identifies himself on Twitter as @MrCruzStar, declared in an interview that the purpose behind these real-time reports is to help minimize the panic among citizens by alerting residents about what parts of the communities to avoid (Rodriguez, 2010). What is more, citizens in these violent areas found in social media the gateway through which they could demand more peace and security for their families and communities (Monroy-Hernandez et al., 2013). Under these circumstances, through social media civilians have established alliances not only with the government, but also with the cartels.[1]

Conclusions

This chapter has outlined the conditions under which social media became a major player in the war on drugs. Despite the initial contributions in the literature, a holistic look at the study of social media usage by drug cartels in Mexico presents some understudied areas. The questions remain: Is social media influence exaggerated? Does it instigate peace or conflict? Is it an instrument that stimulates criminal organizations' power? Can it make criminal organizations more vulnerable? Answers to these questions are still limited.

This chapter highlighted the important role the media has taken in the Mexican war on drugs. It also laid out the evolution of the adoption of new (as opposed to traditional) media becoming a key source for information related to cartels' shootings and blockades. In addition, it suggested that the dynamics among the actors of the drug war changed with the introduction of social media into the equation. In the following chapters, this book attempts to answer the foregoing questions by exploring the effects of the utilization of social media on the Mexican cartels' power and capacity to survive through a comparative analysis of three criminal organizations, the Sinaloa, the Zetas, and the Caballeros Templarios cartels.

Note

1 Examples of the alliances are also explored in Chapter 4.

References

Aday, S., Farrell, H., Lynch, M., Sides, J., Kelly, J., & Zuckerman, E. (2010). *Blogs and bullets: New media in contentious politics*. United States Institute of Peace No. 65.

Adler, I. (1993). The Mexican case: The media in the 1988 presidential election. In T. E. Skidmore (Ed.), *Television, politics, and the transition to democracy in Latin America*. Washington, DC: The Wilson Center and Johns Hopkins University.

Aftergood, S. (2004). *Secrecy news: Social network analysis and intelligence, 15*. Federation of American Scientists Project on Government Secrecy.

Arquilla, J., & Ronfeldt, D. (2001). *Networks and Netwars*. RAND.

Berger, J. M., & Morgan, J. (2015). *Defining and describing the population of ISIS supporters on Twitter*. Brookings. Retrieved from: www.brookings.edu/research/papers/2015/03/isis-twitter-census-berger-morgan.

Castells, M. (2000). *The rise of the networked society*. Cambridge, MA: Blackwell Publishers, Inc.

Cave, D. (2011). Mexico turns to Twitter and Facebook for information and survival. *New York Times*.

Cockrell, C. (2011). *Mexico's new "narcocultura."* Berkeley: University of California.

Correa-Cabrera, G., & Nava, J. (2011). *Drug wars, social networks and the right to information: The rise of informal media as the freedom of press's lifeline in northern Mexico*. APSA 2011 Annual Meeting Paper.

Coscia, M., & Rios, V. (2012). *How and where do criminals operate? Using Google to track Mexican drug trafficking organizations*. Department of Government, Harvard University. Retrieved from: http://scholar.harvard.edu/files/vrios/files/cosciarios_googleforcriminals2.pdf.

Dale, H. (2014). Social media prove double-edged sword for ISIS. *The Daily Signal*. Retrieved from: www.dailysignal.com/2014/10/23/social-media-prove-double-edged-sword-isis/.

Daño Colateral. (2010) *El discurso de Eugenio Hernandez: Del "No pasa nada" a la violencia nos rebaso*. Retrieved from: http://reyno-warrior.blogspot.com/2010/09/el-discurso-de-eugenio-hernandez-del-no.html.

Drezner, D. W., & Farrell, H. (2004). Web of influence. *Foreign Policy*, (145), 32.

Duijn, P. A., Kashirin, V., & Sloot, P. M. (2014). The relative ineffectiveness of criminal network disruption. *Scientific Reports*, 4, 4238.

Eiss, P. K. (2014). The narcomedia. *Latin American Perspectives*, 41(2), 78–98.

Estrin, J. (2011). In Mexico, the glamour of narco-culture. *New York Times*. Retrieved from: https://lens.blogs.nytimes.com/2011/09/02/in-mexico-the-glamor-of-narco-culture/.

Farwell, J. P. (2014). The media strategy of ISIS. *Global Politics and Strategy*, 56(6), 49–55.

Freeman, L. C. (2004). *The development of social network analysis: A study in the sociology of science*. Vancouver, BC: Empirical Press.

Garay Salamanca, L. J., & Salcedo-Albarán, E. (2011). *Drug trafficking corruption and states: How illicit networks reconfigure institutions in Colombia, Guatemala and Mexico*. Bogotá, Colombia: Fundación Método.

Gilsinan, K. (2015). Is ISIS's social-media power exaggerated? *The Atlantic*. Retrieved from: www.theatlantic.com/international/archive/2015/02/is-isiss-social-media-power-exaggerated/385726/.

Giménez-Salinas, A. (2011). *Illegal networks or criminal organizations*. Archives Ceruim: Retrieved from: http://archives.cerium.ca/IMG/pdf/Gimenez_Salinas_Framis_-_Illegal_Networks_Or_Criminal_Organizations.pdf.

Granovetter, M. S. (1973). The strengh of weak ties. *American Journal of Sociology*, 78(6), 1360–1380.

Hallin, D. (2000). Commercialism and professionalism in the American news media. In J. Curran & M. Gurevitch (Eds.), *Mass media and society*. London: Arnold.

Howard, P. N., Duffy, A., Freelon, D., Hussain, M. M., Mari, W., & Marwa, M. (2011). *Opening closed regimes: What was the role of social media during the Arab Spring?* Retrieved from: https://ssrn.com/abstract=2595096 or http://dx.doi.org/10.2139/ssrn.2595096.

International Centre for the Study of Radicalization. (2014). *#GreenBirds: Measuring importance and influence in Syrian foreign fighter networks*. Retrieved from: http://icsr.info/wp-content/uploads/2014/04/ICSR-Report-Greenbirds-Measuring-Importance-and-Infleunce-in-Syrian-Foreign-Fighter-Networks.pdf.

Johnson, N. F., Zhen, M., Vorobyeva, Y., Gabrield, A., Qi, H., Velasquez, N., Manrique, P., Johnson, D., Restrepo, E., Song, C., & Wuchty, S. (2016, June 17). New online ecology of adversarial aggregates: ISIS and beyond. *Science*, 352(6292), 1459–1463.

Jones, N. P. (2016). *The state reaction: A theory of illicit network resilience*. Irvine: University of California.

Kan, P. R. (2013). Cyberwar in the underworld: Anonymous versus Los Zetas in Mexico. *Yale Journal of International Affairs*, 40–51.

Kenney, M. (2007). *From Pablo to Osama: Trafficking and terrorist networks*. Pennsylvania State University Press.

Knoke, D., & Yang, S. (2008). *Social network analysis*. 2nd ed. Series: Quantitative Applications in the Social Sciences. SAGE Publications.

Koschade, S. (2006). A social network analysis of Jemaah Islamiyah: The applications to counterterrorism and intelligence. *Studies in Conflict and Terrorism*, 29(6), 559–575.

Krebs, V. (2002). Mapping networks of terrorists cells. *Connections*, 24(3), 43–52.

La Nación. (2010). En el Blog del Narco todo es crimen y droga. Retrieved from: www.lanacion.com.ar/el-mundo/en-el-blog-del-narco-todo-es-crimen-y-droga-nid1295041.

Lara, T. (2012). *Three Mexican photojournalists found dismembered in Veracruz had been threatened since 2011*. Retrieved from Knight Center for Jounalism in the Americas: https://knightcenter.utexas.edu/blog/00-9998-three-mexican-photojournalists-found-dismembered-veracruz-had-been-threatened-2011.

McAdam, D., Tarrow, S., & Tilly, C. (2001). *Dynamics of contention*. Cambridge University Press.

Medel, M. (2011). *Medios Mexicanos se unen para proteger periodistas y enfrentar propaganda del narcotráfico*. Knight Center for Journalism in the Americas. Retrieved from: https://knightcenter.utexas.edu/es/blog/medios-mexicanos-se-unen-para-proteger-periodistas-y-enfrentar-propaganda-del-narcotrafico.

Monroy-Hernandez, A., boyd, d., Kiciman, E., De Choudhury, M., & Counts, S. (2013). *The new war correspondents: The rise of civic media curation in urban warfare*. Social Networks During Major Transitions. February 23–27, San Antonio, TX.

Morozov, E. (2009). Moldova's Twitter revolution. *Foreign Policy*. Retrieved from: http://neteffect.foreignpolicy.com/posts/2009/04/07/moldovas_twitter_revolution.

Morselli, C. (2009). *Inside criminal networks*. Montreal: Springer.

Müller, M. G., & Hübner, C. (2014). How Facebook facilitated the Jasmine Revolution: Conceptualizing the functions of online social network communication. *Journal of Social Media Studies*, 1(1), 17–33.

Nix, J., Smith, M. R., Petrocelli, M., and Rojek, J. (2016). The use of social media by alleged members of Mexican cartels and affiliated drug trafficking organizations. *Journal of Homeland Security and Emergency Management*, 13(3).

Pereyra, G. (2012). México: Violencia vriminal y "guerra contra el narcotráfico." *Revista Mexicana de Sociología*, 74(3), 429–460.

Renfro, R., & Deckro, R. (2001). *A social network analysis of the Iranian government*. Paper presented at 69th MORS Symposium, 4.

Reuters. (2011). Mexican social media boom draws drug cartel attacks. Retrieved from: www.reuters.com/article/us-mexico-drugs/mexican-social-media-boom-draws-drug-cartel-attacks-idUSTRE78Q6H220110927.

Rodriguez, O. R. (2010). "Blog del Narco" supero la censura en Mexico. *El Mundo*. Retrieved from: www.elmundo.com/portal/pagina.general.impresion.php?idx=156791.

Rothkopf, D. (2015). The paradox of power in the network age. *Foreign Policy*. Retrieved from: http://foreignpolicy.com/2015/10/09/the-network-paradox-islamic-state-nsa-warfare/.

Segerberg, A., & Bennett, W. L. (2011). Social media and the organization of Collective action: Using Twitter to explore the ecologies of two climate change protests. *The Communication Review*, 14(3), 197–215.

Shapiro, C., & Varian, H. R. (1999). *Information rules: A strategic guide to the network economy*. Boston, MA: Harvard Business School Press.

Sparrow, M. (1991). The application of network analysis to criminal intelligence: An assessment of the prospects. *Social Networks, 13*, 251–252.

Stern, J., & Berger, J. M. (2015). *ISIS: The state of terror*. London: William Collins.

Sullivan, A. (2009, June 13). The revolution will be Twittered. *The Atlantic*.

Wagley, J. R. (2006). *Transnational organized crime: Principal threat and U.S. responses*. CRS Report for Congress. Retrieved from: https://fas.org/sgp/crs/natsec/RL33335.pdf.

Waisbord, S. R. (1996). Investigative journalism and political accountability in South American democracies. *Critical Studies in Mass Communication, 13*(4), 343–363.

Wasserman, S., & Faust, K. (1994). *Structural analysis in the social sciences. Social network analysis: Methods and applications*. New York, NY: Cambridge University Press.

World Press Freedom Index. (2018). Reporters without borders for freedom of information. Retrieved from: https://rsf.org/en/ranking/2018.

Chapter 3

The Sinaloa Cartel

Better known for its main leader the infamous Joaquín "El Chapo" Guzmán, the Sinaloa cartel is often listed as one of the largest and most powerful drug trafficking organizations in the world with presence in about 50 countries spread through the U.S., Latin America, Europe, West Africa, South Asia, Australia, and the Philippines. The organization controls between 40 and 60 percent of the total drug trade in Mexico (Congressional Research Service, 2019; InSight Crime, 2016; Beittel, 2013). The territories of their domain consist mainly of five states: Sinaloa, Durango, Chihuahua (also known as "the Golden Triangle"), Baja California, and Sonora. Some estimates indicate that their annual earnings account for about $3 billion (Congressional Research Service, 2019).

The Sinaloa cartel got international attention in 2009 when El Chapo Guzmán made it to the *Forbes'* list as one of the wealthiest people in the world. That same year, *Time* magazine named him one of the "most influential people" under the category of "leaders and revolutionaries," along with President Obama and German Chancellor Angela Merkel (Grayson, 2014). Later, he made the headlines of important journals when he broke out of jail for the second time from a maximum-security prison in Mexico. More recently, and just before his third recapture, he made international headlines once again for his scandalous meeting and interview with Hollywood star Sean Penn and Mexican actress Kate del Castillo. The interview was published in *Rolling Stone* magazine, and the series of text messages between him and the actress regarding a biographical movie deal went viral. This event was the theme of a three-episode series streaming on Netflix, "The Day I Met El Chapo," with Kate del Castillo telling her side of the story. El Chapo's extradition to the U.S. on January 19, 2017, also made headlines worldwide. After these scandals, the organization's popularity on social media grew significantly during the last few years when hashtags such as #*ElChapo* or #*LiberenalChapo* (#*freeElChapo*) became Twitter and Google trending topics. This same year, he was indicted in New York District's federal court in Brooklyn. His court appearances subsequently became a media spectacle and the trial was often called the "trial of the century."

This chapter explores the Sinaloa drug cartel. The first section presents an overall profile of the organization, its history, structure, *modus operandi*, and its current state of affairs. The second section analyses the survival capacity of the organization. Through indicators of violence, to measure cartel presence, I observe how the cartel has responded to organizational shocks. As previously specified, these shocks include the capture or killing of important members. The third section explores the cartel's presence on and usage of social media platforms, followed by analysis and conclusions.

A Cartel Is Born

The Sinaloa cartel, also referred as the Federation or the Blood Alliance, splintered from the Guadalajara cartel in the mid-1980s. The Guadalajara cartel was one of the most powerful in the country and was commanded by Miguel Angel Félix Gallardo "El Padrino" (the Godfather). In 1989, the Mexican authorities captured Félix Gallardo, and consequently the cartel disintegrated. The remaining leaders of the cartel met in Acapulco, Guerrero. By the end of the gathering, the Tijuana, Beltrán Leyva, and Sinaloa cartel were born. They divided the territories and assigned trafficking routes to each cartel. The new rules of the game were simple: respect the turf of counterparts (both friends and enemies) and comply with the tacit agreements between them and the government (Keefe, 2012). On the years to come, these cartels would become implacable enemies and the protagonists of bloody turf wars.

The state of Sinaloa has been the ancestral land and cradle of the most famous narco legends in Mexico such as Rafael Caro Quintero, Miguel Angel Félix Gallardo, Ernesto Fonseca Carrillo, and Héctor Luis "El Güero" Palma. Lying between the *Sierra Madre Occidental* and Mexico's west coast, the state's topography embraces vast mountainous territories and fertile grounds. Here, the crops of marijuana and poppy grow easily and can simply be hidden. Their geographical location, often called the "opium central," makes the area ideal for transportation and logistics for drug trafficking.

Structure and Modus Operandi

The cartel of Sinaloa is configured as a "federation" rather than a vertical, top-down syndicate. Experts also call this structure "hub-and-spokes" (InSight Crime, 2016). In this kind of organization, power is not concentrated only in one person at the top of a pyramid; instead, various leaders share control. The Sinaloa cartel was founded and managed by four main drug lords: "El Chapo" Guzmán, Ismael "El Mayo" Zambada García, Juan José Esparragoza Moreno "El Azul," and Ignacio "El Nacho" Coronel. These associates worked in conjunction, but at the same time enjoyed a degree of autonomy. They had leverage to function on their own and conduct their operations separately (Grayson, 2014).

The organization's *modus operandi* is based on cohesion and an intrinsic web of bribery of politicians, police, judges, and prosecutors. The cartel dominates traffic routes from the northwest of Mexico to Central America and controls important traffic points. The organization has distinguished itself for its eclectic and sophisticated methods for trafficking drugs. It uses planes (commercial and private), container ships, fishing vessels, boats, and submarines to transfer the illegal drugs across borders. In addition, it uses catapults, cannons, and the famous tunnels at the U.S.–Mexico border.

The Cartel Today

The cartel has lost most of its main leaders. The only one standing is Ismael "El Mayo" Zambada, and maybe Juan José Esparragoza "El Azul," who is presumed to have died from a heart attack in 2014, though his death was never made official. The other key leader, Ignacio "El Nacho" Coronel, was killed by the Mexican army in 2010, and El Chapo was captured again on January 16, 2016. It is believed that his second escape from a maximum-security federal prison in Mexico in 2015 was a major embarrassment for Peña Nieto and influenced the decision to accept the drug lord's extradition to the U.S. early in 2017 (Congressional Research Service, 2019). El Chapo's trial lasted four months. In July 2019, he was sentenced to life in prison, with an additional 30 years, and he was ordered to pay $12.6 billion in forfeiture for his leadership in the cartel (Congressional Research Service, 2019).

There has been much speculation about the future of the organization without El Chapo. Many experts agree that his arrest will not much change or affect the performance of the cartel. The reason is that the network the organization has created is so intrinsic that, even without his leadership, the smuggling infrastructure is likely to endure regardless of who takes his place (Keefe, 2012). Another reason why the criminal organization remains powerful is the cartel's establishment in other countries (Congressional Research Service, 2019). El Mayo continues to operate the organization along with Guzmán's sons Alfredo and Ivan Archivaldo Guzmán (Janowitz, 2016).

With El Chapo incarcerated, there have been signs of intra-cartel rupture and generational tensions. The repartition of El Chapo's domains led to conflict between the Guzmán brothers and Dámaso López "El Mini Lic," fighting for Guzmán's legacy. It is believed that El Mini Lic was behind the kidnapping of Alfredo Guzmán by Cartel Jalisco Nueva Generación (releasing him days after) and also other attacks against Guzmán's family. After this event, frictions between the two counterparts started to intensify (*Excélsior*, 2017). In July 2017, Dámaso López turned himself in to U.S. authorities at a port of entry into the state of California. Since then, he has denounced more than 125 accomplices of the cartel, which has negatively affected the criminal organization (Woody, 2017). Moreover, there have also been disagreements between the *narcojuniors*[1] and the veterans, especially El Mayo Zambada, about the way the *narcojuniors* are running their part of the business. These circumstances point to tensions within the organization, which may lead to fragmentation in the future. In October 2019, El Chapo's son Ovidio Guzmán was detained by the state police in Culiacán, Sinaloa. The event created chaos in the city, brought about by members of the cartel in order to cause commotion, with the promise to create more commotion, pressuring the security forces to release Ovidio, which they did.

Despite these important setbacks, the organization remains powerful, expanding over the Mexican territory and seeking new market opportunities in other countries such as China, Japan, and Australia. The Ovidio incident sheds light on several issues, including the influence the cartel has over the state, and the transition of the Sinaloa cartel from a traditional to a non-traditional criminal organization.

Survival Capacity: A Fierce Organization

The Sinaloa cartel has suffered important disruptions, but these have not significantly affected the solidity of the organization. In Chapter 2, I discussed some possible explanations for this, including economic, social, cultural, and exogenous factors. Nevertheless, all the other drug cartels in Mexico share the same conditions. So, what makes the Sinaloa cartel more resistant than others?

In order to address the question, this section examines the survival capacity of the cartel. The first part presents the cartel's clashes, how much it fights and with whom. The second presents a model assessing its level of violence (homicides) and criminal activities (kidnappings, and extortions), and its response to organizational shocks.

The Confrontations

The relative peace the cartels enjoyed for many years started to be disrupted once the PAN took office under President Vicente Fox's mandate in 2000. With the party transition, a new drug trafficking landscape arose and new cartels were created that started to violate the established agreements. Until the military became involved in the counter-drug efforts, violent clashes detonated all over the Mexican territory. This section explores the clashes the Sinaloa cartel has faced during the war years. I monitored and coded all news involving the Sinaloa cartel reported on *El Universal* from 2006 to 2015. The reports chosen for the analysis denote only the ones containing detailed information about the confrontations in which members of the Sinaloa cartel were involved. *El Universal*'s archives contained 4,831 news items related to

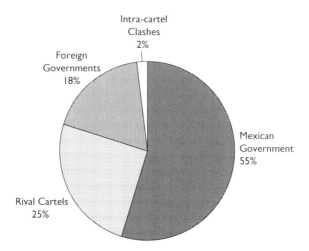

Graph 3.1 Sinaloa Cartel's Reported Clashes 2006–2015.

the Sinaloa cartel, only 305 of which were about confrontations in which the cartel was involved. The analysis below is based on those notes. Graph 3.1 illustrates the shares of conflicts the cartel has faced from 2006 to 2015.

The graph shows that more than half of the attacks and confrontations of the cartel were against the Mexican government.[2] The second greatest group consists of rival cartels, especially the Zetas and the Juárez cartel, more in particular with its armed wing "La Línea," making up 25 percent of the clashes the cartel has experienced since 2006. Foreign governments account for 18 percent of the confrontations. Most of the attacks from external governments have been executed by the U.S. security forces, reported mostly in the state of Arizona. Other countries include: Colombia, Costa Rica, Chile, Ecuador, Guatemala, Honduras, Nicaragua, Panama, the Netherlands, Argentina, the Philippines, and Spain. In recent years, the involvement of foreign governments has increased. This may be an indicator that the cartel has established strong roots, or opened new routes and markets in those countries, or maybe a more aggressive anti-drug strategy has been adopted by other countries.

Overall, these clashes have led to the loss of many lives, including narcos, security forces, and innocent people. Some of these battles have caused harm within the organization as well. The bloody conflicts take place within urban areas at any time of the day or night, or others occur in remote places where the noise of battle echoes around the mountains and the bullet-riddled bodies find their final resting places.

Most of the combats in which the cartel has been a participant concentrate on the states of Sinaloa, Baja California, and Chihuahua, followed by Jalisco and Mexico City. The data also shows that the cartel's quarrels have varied throughout the drug war years, that they have fought with some rivals more than others, and that some years have been awfully violent and others relatively more peaceful. For example, in 2006, the organization was mainly targeted by the Mexican army. During 2008, it was targeted more specifically by the federal police. The year 2010 was extremely violent: the cartel was constantly targeted by the Mexican army, federal, and local police. This same year, the Zetas separated from the Gulf cartel and started to expand their territories, causing an escalation of brutal confrontations. Starting in 2012, the cartel underwent more attacks in foreign countries. It is also apparent that the Mexican marines became their worst enemy during 2015, and that they fight the most during the summer months.

This section has demonstrated that the Sinaloa cartel has been constantly targeted by different actors, foreign and domestic, during the last decade. How has the cartel been able to survive and remain strong under constant attacks? Next, I explore the way the cartel has reacted towards clashes resulting in significant setbacks to the organization.

Major Organizational Shocks and the Sinaloa Cartel's Response

As mentioned earlier, throughout the drug war years, the cartel has suffered significant disruptions. Such disturbances range from the demise of cells in Mexico and other countries, to important seizures of shipments of drugs, weapons, ammunition, and money, and to the destruction of clandestine labs to process drugs, and of the drug crops themselves, among others. One of the most important setbacks the Sinaloa cartel has suffered is the capture of Joaquín "El Chapo" Guzmán. Then again, even under these harsh circumstances, being constantly attacked and without one of its most important leaders, the organization continues to operate. This section aims to examine the most significant organizational setbacks the cartel has encountered and its reaction to them.

In October 2008, one of the "triumphs" of the administration of Felipe Calderón was the arrest of Jesús Reynaldo Zambada García "El Rey." El Mayo Zambada's brother stood as a central piece in the structure of the cartel. He oversaw the criminal activities in the Mexican Valley and was responsible for the production of massive quantities of methamphetamines in clandestine laboratories, and for the import of cocaine precursors from South American countries through Mexico City's international airport (Fox, 2012).

According to Grayson (2014), another significant shock the cartel suffered was the capture, in 2009, of Vicente Zambada Niebla "El Vicentillo," El Mayo's son, by the federal police in a suburb outside Mexico City. Five hours before his detention, Zambada Niebla had met with the DEA. El

Vicentillo was in charge of coordinating the shipment of tons of cocaine into the U.S. He was extradited to the northern country in 2010.

An additional noteworthy disruption suffered by the Sinaloa cartel was the assassination of Ignacio Coronel "El Nacho" Villarreal, third in command of the cartel until his murder by the Mexican army in June of 2010. He controlled a broad coastal strip that includes the states of Jalisco, Colima, Nayarit, and a part of Michoacán. El Nacho had direct access to cocaine suppliers in Colombia, and established a chain of supply from Asia to traffic precursors needed to produce methamphetamines.

Two years later in 2012, Manuel Torres Félix "El Ondeado" or "M-1" was killed during a violent clash with the Mexican army. He was a high-ranking leader who oversaw drug trafficking shipments from South America into Mexico. He was the right hand of El Mayo and a major administrative figure in the organization. There is some controversy about the death of this important member since some conspiracy theories state that El Mayo supposedly set him up with the Mexican government (Ramsey, 2012).

The next two years would be harsh for the organization as it lost three important members. In 2013, Gabíno Salas Valenciano "El Ingeniero" in charge of the Juárez *plaza*, a key territory for trafficking, was assassinated. This same year, José Rodrigo Aréchiga "El Chino Antrax" was captured in Brussels, in an operation led by Interpol and the Dutch police (*Excélsior*, 2014). El Chino Antrax started in the organization as a professional hitman. He later formed and managed the armed wing "Los Antrax" in charge of the security for El Mayo. The organization invested significantly in this group to get them highly trained and they later served as an important part of the cartel (Milenio, 2014).

The last shock considered here, and the most vital to date, is the arrest of El Chapo Guzmán in 2014. As is known, he escaped in July 2015 and was recaptured about six months later in early 2016. El Chapo's capture in 2014 was chosen for the analysis since it counts as the last significant shock to the organization within the scope of this research.

Some believe that in June 2014, one of the four main leaders of the cartel "El Azul" died from a heart attack. This would have been another setback of great magnitude for the cartel. Nevertheless, the drug lord could be faking his death once again. Many experts consider he is still alive and managing the cartel along with El Mayo. Since his death is not official, it is not considered in this study.

Figure 3.1 illustrates a time line for when these major setbacks took place and how the cartel responded based on their criminal activities.

The model shows that the Sinaloa cartel's criminal activities have fluctuated throughout the years and that they have reacted differently towards organizational shocks. Theory suggests that after a top leader of a criminal organization is removed, violence will erupt, indicating a time of

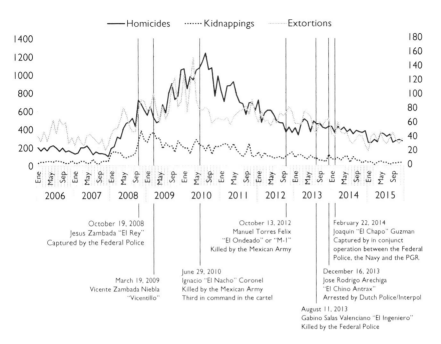

Figure 3.1 Sinaloa Cartel's Response to Organizational Shocks 2006–2015.

re-accommodation and restructuring within a criminal group. We can see this trend happening with the Sinaloa cartel, as increases in violence after every seizure can be observed, but the response is more prominent in some cases more than others.

After the capture of "El Rey" in 2008, and "El Vicentillo" the following year, an increase of criminal activities and violence is evident. Later in 2010, the indicators reach a peak soon after the assassination of Nacho Coronel. The DEA called the Coronel's death "a crippling blow" to the organization (Ellingwood, 2010). The absence of this leader really affected the Sinaloa cartel. His death sparked major turf wars in Guadalajara involving major cartels and allied gangs (Grayson, 2014). The escalation of violence may be an indicator of intra-cartel conflicts or confrontations with rival groups. The Juárez cartel attempted to take over the Coronel's domains, which led to an increase in battles between these two criminal organizations.

This analysis suggests that after these three significant losses in the organization, more precisely after the death of El Nacho Coronel, the cartel faced a turbulent period during which it was forced to make important structural changes. The latter are reflected in the way the organization reacts to the disruptions that follow. After the restructuring process, the cartel seems to be more solid, showing more congruence when facing new disturbances.

After the reconfiguration, indicators of violence and criminal activities remain relatively steady after key shocks.

During the following years, violence in their areas of influence slowly started to go down. The organizational shocks suffered in 2012 and two in 2013 (El M-1, El Ingeniero, and El Chino Antrax respectively) do not show significant impact on their criminal activities. Later, on February 22, 2014, the most powerful capo in the world Joaquín "El Chapo" Guzmán was captured in a joint operation between the federal police, the Navy, and the PGR. Being the main known leader of the organization there was a lot of speculation about how the organization was going to react and an increase of violence was of course expected. Strangely, El Chapo's capture does not show much impact on the cartel's criminal activities. There are two possible explanations for this: the first is that during the restructuring period the organization became more solid, organized, and stronger. The second is that by that time, El Chapo did not have as much influence in the organization as before, and his influence in the decision-making process of the cartel had diminished. In the next section, this possibility is further explored.

The Sinaloa Cartel on Social Media

Social media has changed the way we communicate. One of its key features is that anyone with internet access can connect with others without intermediaries and it offers a degree of anonymity. Web platforms such as Twitter have made possible one-on-one interactions, so now it is feasible to directly tweet or send a message to a favorite artist, state leaders like President Obama, or Trump, or even to the most well-known drug lord since Pablo Escobar, El Chapo Guzmán.

Members of the Sinaloa cartel have extensively used social media and their presence on these platforms is significant. As mentioned in Chapter 1, the use of social media by criminal and terrorist organizations has given them worldwide exposure. Although members of these groups are present on several social media platforms such as Instagram, or Snapchat, this study focuses on the cartel's use of Twitter and YouTube.[3] What follows is a detailed analysis of the cartel on these communication channels.

Online Presence

The Sinaloa cartel holds a wide-ranging fan base on social media. Just in Twitter, the universe of their network is about 140 million people. They have followers from all over the world, including the U.S., Ecuador, Colombia, Venezuela, Uruguay, Peru, Argentina, Turkey, and of course Mexico. To locate the most important nodes, actors, or accounts in their vast network, I conducted a social network analysis (SNA) of the Sinaloa cartel's Twitter

The Sinaloa Cartel 61

network; this also helped in constructing a visual picture of their online network configuration.

The social network of the cartel presented here is a simplification of their network since it only considers the most relevant nodes. In other words, it is based on the nodes with more interaction and linkages among them. This simplified version of the network comprises a total of 353 main nodes with 5,066 edges or links. The analysis started with El Chapo's official Twitter account and then other accounts were gradually added so as to have a more comprehensive scheme. Two main measures of centrality were considered to determine the most important nodes: in-degree and betweenness.[4] These metrics are helpful to determine the importance and quality of a node in a network in terms of connecting individuals or groups. Nodes with high a degree of betweenness function as intermediaries. Their role is important because without them, communication between actors, modules, or groups can be broken or nonexistent. In addition, I used the modularity function to find commonalities or groups within the network. Modularity is a measure to detect communities in large networks. Networks with high modularity have denser connections between the nodes within modules but sparse connections between the nodes in diverse modules (Xiaonan, Machiraju, Ritter, & Yen, 2015). Other factors considered when choosing the accounts analyzed for this case study were the number of followers and specific content. Graph 3.2 is an approximate visualization of the Sinaloa cartel Twitter network.

There is a great amount of information that can be construed from the SNA. In the Graph 3.2, it can be observed that the Twitter network structure of the Sinaloa cartel bears a resemblance to its physical configuration. In other words, it is similar to a hub-and-spokes structure. The network is divided into five main modules or groups. The groups labeled G3 and G4 on the graph do not tell us much about their structure, but they give information about the cartel members' personal interests. For instance, we can see that they are interested in following Mexican president Enrique Peña Nieto, and they like to be informed since they present reciprocal connections with numerous news outlets. The graph also shows that they have interests in international politics, following the accounts of former U.S. presidential candidate Hillary Clinton and now President Donald Trump, and of some governmental institutions from Colombia. They are soccer aficionados, like Pitbull's music, and are Playboy fans.

Group 2 (G2) is directly related to El Chapo Guzmán, being his "official" account, the most central node of the entire network. After him, the accounts of his sons Alfredo, Ivan, and Ovidio Guzmán follow in importance and centrality, and then accounts of members with lower positions on the organizational ladder. Group 1 (G1) represents a group conformed by various armed wings of the cartel: *la Gente Nueva*, *Los Antrax*, *los Damaso*, *los 701*, and a group led by El Gallito called *los 12*. Group 3 (G3) is formed by El Mayo Zambada and his closest constituents, though this is a much

62 The Sinaloa Cartel

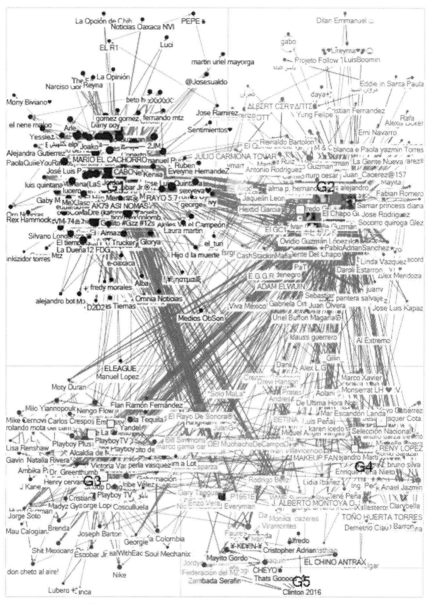

Created with NodeXL Pro (http://nodexl.codeplex.com) from the Social Media Research Foundation (http://www.smrfoundation.org)

Graph 3.2 Sinaloa Cartel's Twitter Network.

Source: Created with NodeXL Pro (http://nodexl.codeplex.com) from the Social Media Research Foundation (www.smrfoundation.org)

smaller cluster. The groups are connected only through a few nodes that link the network together.

There are behavioral patterns that these accounts follow, depending on their centrality. Highly central nodes such as El Chapo, his sons, and El Mayo Zambada use an open–close system to communicate through the network, serving mainly as sources of information. In other words, they post messages, receive likes and comments, but rarely answer or engage in conversations. These nodes have a particular characteristic, which is that they are followed by thousands of people but they only follow and interact with a small set of nodes. For example, El Chapo's Twitter account has 610,376 followers whereas he only follows 17 people, mostly family members. His son Ivan Archivaldo follows only 35 accounts, and he is followed by 323,387 Twitter users. His brother Alfredo follows only five persons, but he is followed by 310,700. Nodes with less centrality throughout the network follow and are followed by more accounts promoting interaction with their followers. In Group 1 (G1), this type of behavior is observed the most.

In a similar fashion, there is also a resemblance in how El Chapo and El Mayo and the groups under their leadership behave online and offline. For example, El Chapo and the groups under his command, especially the *narcojuniors*, like to be public, popular, and controversial on social media just as they are loud, extravagant, and irreverent in their real lives. El Mayo Zambada instead maintains a low profile, on social media as well, using the platforms just "to inform the truth" about the cartel. He follows only one account and writes posts that are discrete about his life and whereabouts, but, at the same time, contain encrypted and detailed information about the organization's status. As in the virtual plane, in real life, El Mayo Zambada has always maintained a low profile, which has helped him avoid detection by the authorities during his 40 years or more in the business.

Even though these accounts contain highly graphic violent content, just a few of them have been taken down by the social media platform. During the time I studied these accounts, I only encountered three cases of accounts that were closed, and then reopened with a different user name. The content of the social media accounts of members of ISIS and members of the Mexican cartel are not that different. ISIS's accounts, nonetheless, are constantly attacked and taken down (Johnson et al., 2016); this is not the case with the members of cartels in Mexico.

Twitter and YouTube's Content Analysis

The information members of the cartel provide on social media is vast in scale, impressively detailed, sweet, humane, violent, and horrific. Going through the content of their accounts is a roller coaster of emotions. The visuals on these webpages range from love letters to decapitated bodies. The nature of the content of their posts has brought them international attention, making the Sinaloa cartel members popular personalities, with celebrity-like status. It has also made them accessible to the public, and more relatable.

Through their accounts, they let us contemplate the stories from their own point of view, giving us direct access to their life in the underworld. They present a different metanarrative on the cartel. Below, the analysis of the content of their Twitter accounts and YouTube videos is presented.

Twitter

Most journalistic articles and research done on the content of narcos' social media accounts have mainly focused on the ostentatious lifestyle members of cartels show on their pages. There is so much more information worth exploring. I uncovered 12 different categories based on the content of their posts. These categories include: description about their operations and missions, pictures/videos depicting their luxurious lifestyle, threatening messages, altruism, and recruitment. They also update their followers about the status of the organization, and communicate with each other through posting coded messages on their walls. Graph 3.3 illustrates the breakdown of their usage.

Tweets about their missions and operations account for 25 percent of the content of the accounts. On these posts, phrases like "mission accomplished" or "following orders" are common along with photos or videos of them before, during, or after the job was completed. In these images, they show entire convoys of trucks in action, and the members dress in military-style uniforms and proudly hold AK-15 rifles, ready to complete their task. Another portion of these posts contains videos of training camps, and uploads of footage of actual confrontations, displaying the corpses of enemies that died during a battle to intimidate adversaries.

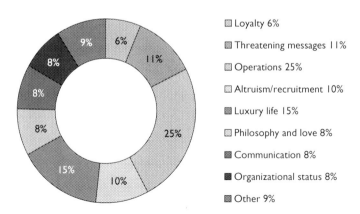

Graph 3.3 Sinaloa Cartel's Twitter Content Analysis.

In some of the videos, they can be seen working or moving cargoes at Mexican air force military bases. This suggests that the cartel has a close relationship with some of the Mexican security forces. They also upload pictures of their business trips. A good number of these posts come from cities in the U.S. such as Los Angeles and Chicago, which are known distribution hubs. They do state that they upload the pictures days or weeks after their visits to prevent operations being tracked. In several posts, they mention that their armed groups and cartel members get specialized training in the Middle East, in partnership with Al Qaeda and ISIS.

Probably the most common and studied posts of the cartel on social media are the ones related to their luxurious lifestyle. Although this study shows that it is not the main purpose of their social media use, this category takes the second place with 15 percent. Members of the cartel – and especially the *narcojuniors*, such as Alfredo and Ivan Archivaldo Guzmán, El Chayo, or El Mini Lic (before he self-surrendered) – post pictures with bales of money, drugs, gold-plated weapons, trips, planes, boats, Bentleys, Lamborghinis, Ferraris, ostentatious parties, fine jewelry, brand clothing, beautiful women, and exotic pets. In other words, they present to their followers a dream lifestyle, which attracts especially impressionable young people.

The cartels also use these communication platforms to send threatening messages to other rival organizations and to the government. These types of messages account for 11 percent of the content. The menacing posts for other cartels mainly claim territories, bragging about a victorious battle, and showing pictures of rival cartel members massacred. They send messages to the government declaring that the marines are being abusive to civilians, killings innocent civilians including children, directly tagging government agencies such as SEMAR (the Marines Secretariat) on their posts. After El Chapo's last capture, his son Alfredo posted threatening messages to the government implying that the person responsible for the arrest would face horrid consequences: "the government will pay for this betrayal, one should never bite the hand that feeds you," he wrote. They have also posted threats tagging President Peña Nieto, the Secretary of National Defense (SEDENA), and members of rival cartels directly. El Chapo's account posted a message to Donald Trump's account *@realDonaldTrump* threatening him after a series of invidious speeches targeting Mexicans.

Other purposes of use include altruistic propaganda and recruitment, with 10 percent of the content. "We protect and support the cartel [Sinaloa], we are at the service of the community and with the people," reads the opening line of the Twitter account of *Gente del Chapo* (Chapo's people), one cell of El Chapo's faction. Such propaganda might help the cartel to legitimize their business and gain acceptance from society. What is more, these accounts get job petitions from followers posting their requests on their public walls. These include profiles of citizens working in the formal sector, some with university degrees such as lawyers and accountants. Employment seekers usually post comments complaining about their low income, inability to provide enough to their families, and distrust in the government. Cartel members usually respond by asking them to send their resumes through the inbox. Another recruitment strategy of cartel members is to create groups through the WhatsApp application and ask their followers to post their cellphone numbers in order to be added to a group. These types of messages seem to be effective since they commonly get between 300 and 400 responses from followers providing their personal information.

The cartel uses social media to talk about the status of the organization when changes are taking place (8 percent). For example, when El Chapo was taken by the authorities in 2016, cartel members announced through their Twitter accounts who was replacing him. The message was posted on the official page of the cartel @CartelDSinaloa on March 8, 2016, a few weeks after the capo's capture, and read as follows: "The new leaders of the Sinaloa Cartel: @IvanArchivaldo with his brother @_AlfredoGuzman_ will have the control of the cartel."

The criminal organization's members also use social media platforms to communicate with each other during missions. They do this by posting coded messages on their walls and then tagging each other. These types of posts account for 8 percent of their content. Finally, 14 percent of their posts show a more human side of the drug traffickers. They write love letters, they post about their philosophy on life, and they profess an enormous amount of respect, pride, and loyalty to the Sinaloa cartel and its leaders.

YouTube

When one types "cartel de Sinaloa" in the YouTube search bar, 99,100 videos are found. For the purpose of this research, I used the "most relevant" filter

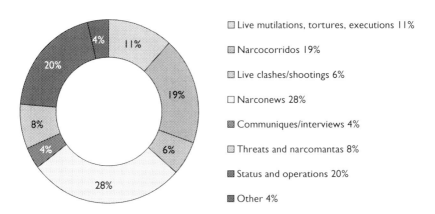

Graph 3.4 Sinaloa Cartel's YouTube Content Analysis.

option and got 578 videos ranging from 800 to more than 1.5 million views. Graph 3.4 presents a classification of the content of the videos.

The presence of the Sinaloa cartel in YouTube differs a bit from Twitter. Most of the videos in this portal are related to *narconews*, which accounts for 28 percent of the content. Some of these news clips come from national or regional televised newscasts, but the majority come from videos posted in *Blog del Narco*.[5] The videos that come from the latter webpage present detailed information about the cartels, sometimes information not found in any journal, newscast, book, or article, or on other social media platforms. Such information includes messages warning the population about possible violent events, interviews with cartel members talking about the general situation of the Sinaloa cartel, their alliances, main rivalries, and future endeavors. Similarly, there are messages detailing the involvement of government officials in the cartel's activities.

The next category, with 20 percent, covers the Sinaloa cartel's use of YouTube to inform the public about their missions or operations, including some videos in which members of the cartel explain in more depth how the organization works. In these messages, they describe more in detail that their organization has a Council Board that takes the important decisions. The board is responsible for deciding whether they will take El Chapo once again out of jail or they will opt for his extradition, for example. In addition, they describe in detail how the leaders of the main cartels in Mexico have organized conclaves to reestablish the new rules of the game, to stop the chaos and extreme violence, since it was starting to affect the business. According to an audio in one of the videos, the first meeting happened in June 2007, in a ranch owned by Heriberto Lazcano near Valle Hermoso, in the state of Tamaulipas. The main leaders of the drug cartels at the time, El Chapo, Vicente Carrillo Fuentes, Juan José Esparragoza Moreno, Ismael Zambada, Ignacio Coronel, Arturo and Héctor Beltrán Leyva, and Heriberto Lazcano, got together to discuss issues including the repartition of territories, the accommodation of new cartels, and the cessation of violence that had got out of control. In the meeting, resolutions were made just for a short period of time since "El Lazca" (leader of the Zetas at the time) did not agree to some of the rules established, nor did he trust his enemies.[6] More meetings were held later in Cuernavaca, Morelos, and Polanco in Mexico City.

Following this, with 19 percent of the content, are *narcocorridos*. The *narcocorridos* have played a key role in the diffusion of a narcoculture in Mexico. These are songs that narrate the life or epic stories of a drug lord or an organization. Usually the lyrics describe the drug traffickers as legendary heroes and idolize the lifestyle. This music genre became popular in Mexico especially during the war. It is believed that *narcocorridos* incite violence and increase the popularity of the narcoculture.

The content in YouTube videos related to the Sinaloa cartel is highly graphic. Their cruelty sometimes surpasses fiction in horror films; 11 percent of the content is footage of live tortures and execution style killings. The purpose of these horrible videos is to intimidate rival cartels and to extract information from the victims. The remaining elements of the content are threats directed to the government and other cartels with 8 percent, followed by videos of live battles and shootings with 6 percent. The last 4 percent corresponds to communiques about the cartel's endeavors and some interviews.

The Untold Story of the Sinaloa Cartel

Twitter accounts and YouTube videos of the Sinaloa cartel underline a story very different from the one commonly known about the criminal organization on mainstream media. The content on social media almost takes the reader or viewer into a parallel world of the cartel, in which, if examined meticulously, a different perspective than the one put forward into public view can be perceived.

One of the more interesting accounts studied here is allegedly managed by El Mayo Zambada (@mzoficial).[7] According to him, he passed down his account to the new leaders taking his place from what is now called "the MZ Federation," after he "retired" in 2013. Supposedly, he now works just as the advisor to the organization. On this Twitter account, another version of the way the cartel operates is revealed. Here, it is stated that, contrary to common knowledge, El Chapo had not been the most powerful member of the Sinaloa cartel in recent years, but he had been chosen to be the public figure of the organization. In other words, El Chapo served as a façade to distract attention from the real leader of the cartel, El Mayo Zambada. In these accounts, they discuss how Rafael Caro Quintero or "Mr. from the 80s" came back as a leader of the cartel once he was released from prison at the beginning of Peña Nieto's administration in 2012, serving mostly as an advisor.[8]

In his alleged account, El Mayo or his proxies imply that the cartel's power goes beyond the Mexican government. They claim that the leaders of the Sinaloa cartel are the ones who choose who will be the presidents not only of Mexico, but also of other countries in South America. Through his account, El Mayo communicates that, in conjunction with higher officials, they had chosen the next Mexican president who started in 2018 ("one more radical").

Finally, some other posts talk about conflicts and treason within the organization. They narrate that the General Council of the cartel decided to turn El Chapo over to the authorities in 2014. The reasons behind the decision included indiscipline and excesses, from him and the groups he was leading.[9] One element of this misconduct was related to their overexposure on social media. El Chapo continued with this behavior even after his second escape in 2015, hence the Sean Penn and Kate del

The Sinaloa Cartel 69

Castillo scandal. According to El Mayo's account, such behavior represents a danger to the cartel and does not comply with the rules of the organization.

Social Media Use and Organizational Shocks

In the previous section, I presented a model to assess the survival capacity of the Sinaloa cartel; here the framework is used to observe the cartel's behavior on social media after each organizational shock.[10] Figure 3.2 shows that two years after the media censorship in the country took place, the presence of the Sinaloa cartel on Twitter displays a significant increase. Organizational disruptions are notoriously reflected in their social media use, which peaks after most of these events.

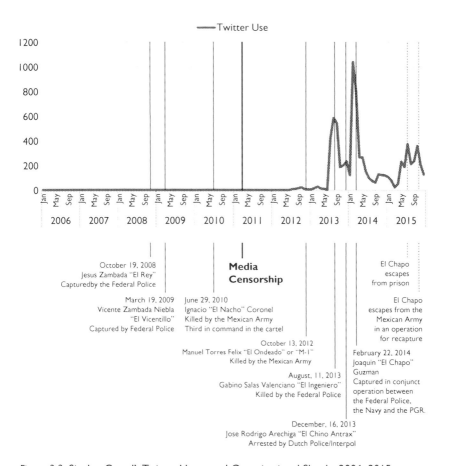

Figure 3.2 Sinaloa Cartel's Twitter Usage and Organizational Shocks 2006–2015.

Their Twitter usage exploded during the capture of El M-1 and of course El Chapo in 2014. The model shows that the cartel members' usage of social media increases when the organization experiences organizational shocks. The messages uploaded during these events correspond to posts giving information about the state of the organization during and after a disruption, and also sending threats to the ones responsible for the attack.

The Analysis

The purpose of this project is to study whether or not the implementation of social media in their strategies has helped strengthen drug trafficking organizations in Mexico. The data presented in this chapter suggests that the Sinaloa cartel's survival capacity has remained strong, responding differently to organizational shocks throughout the years. Nevertheless, going back to my assumptions the question remains: is the use of social media by the cartels beneficial to their survival capacity? Or, to the contrary, does it make them more exposed and vulnerable? To address the questions, social media usage activity and the reported clashes are analyzed. Graph 3.5 illustrates the relationship between the two variables.

One of the hypotheses this study presents is that an increase in the usage of social media will lead to more attacks against an organization since exposure on these communication outlets can increase their detectability, making them more vulnerable. A statistical correlation between Twitter usage and reported clashes shows a negative relationship. What is more, the Pearson's correlation coefficient does not show any statistical significance, indicating that the relationship between these two variables is weak.

Correspondingly, a regression was used to assess the explanatory power between clashes and social media use. The results in Table 3.1 show a positive correlation between the two variables, but it is not a significant one.

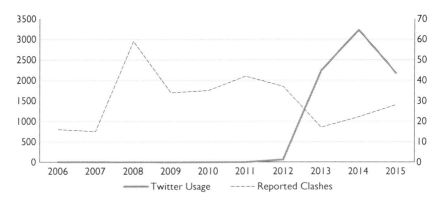

Graph 3.5 Sinaloa Cartel's Twitter Usage and Reported Clashes 2006–2015.

Table 3.1 Sinaloa Cartel Regression, Clashes and Social Media Use

Model Summary

Model	R	R Square	Adjusted R Square	Std. Error of the Estimate
1	0.003[a]	0.000	−0.008	2.620

Note
a. Predictors: (Constant), Twitter.

The probability that social media has a causal effect on the organization's clashes is nonexistent. As shown through the analysis in this chapter, the cartel makes use of social media platforms widely, and exploits them even more when it experiences organizational blows.

Conclusions

There is a theory that argues that the Sinaloa cartel has a high capacity for survival and maintains its power due to the fact that the government favors the organization over the others. This would mean that the military or other judicial bodies do not target the cartel as much since it is protected by the deeply corrupted system the organization has created. The reported clashes gathered in this study show that from 2006 to 2015 the organization was constantly targeted by Mexican security forces, security from other countries, and rival cartels. In fact, according to a recount published by *El Universal*, between 2013 and 2015 the Sinaloa cartel was the criminal organization that suffered the most arrests in comparison with the other Mexican criminal organizations.[11]

The cartel's use of social media is extensive, and their posts share a lot of information about their criminal organization. In this chapter, I have presented a social network analysis to discover the more relevant accounts in the Sinaloa cartel's Twitter network and to visualize its structure. When exploring their network, it is noticeable that the nodes with the highest degree of centrality serve as informants, the nodes with the higher degree of betweenness function as disseminators of information, and they are the nodes that links the network together.

The analysis in this case suggests that although important members of the cartel, especially the *narcojuniors*, are highly exposed on these outlets, and though some of them have been captured, there is no evidence that the cartel has been weakened because of social media use. Indeed, it is observed that notable members and leaders of this organization are cynically too exposed in these platforms such as the sons of El Chapo, Alfredo and Ivan Archivaldo Guzmán, and they are still holding leadership position in the organization.

In a counterfactual scenario, would the Sinaloa cartel remain strong without social media? Probably, yes, but to what degree is hard to assess. There are factors that social media has helped to strengthen and facilitate for the organization. The degree of narcoculture penetration during the last few years in the country might not have been possible without these communication outlets. Social media has aided the cartel to be closer, more reachable, and relatable to the citizenry, and this closeness might help in building social acceptance and support. As the literature suggests, social and cultural acceptability is key for the successful functionality of criminal organizations. Another important factor that social media has facilitated is recruitment. These platforms have eased the way to find new people interested in working for the cartel, and in fact, as was found in the content analysis, people usually reach out to them looking for employment. The rapid replacement of killed or arrested members is important to maintain a stable system.

Finally, the SNA demonstrated that the cartel's virtual constitution is reminiscent of their physical one, reflecting a hub-and-spokes structure. This will be helpful in identifying central nodes or some structural holes in the virtual arena that can assist with recognizing weaknesses in their structure. Alternative strategies, besides the kingpin, can be developed to disrupt the organization. The kingpin strategy or high-value targeting having proven ineffective, it might be possible that a *from-within* strategy might work better than a top-down approach, or, as Felbad-Brown proposes, a middle-level targeting and focused-deterrence approach "would be more effective policy choices" (2013: p. 2). The author further states that "focusing law enforcement on the middle layer of criminal groups tends to be more effective in incapacitating groups and reducing violence ... [it] limits the leadership regeneration capacity of the group" (Felbad-Brown, 2013: p. 10).

Notes

1 *Narcojuniors* is a term used to refer to the children of older drug traffickers. Unlike their parents, they have been raised in wealth. They like to expose themselves and their exuberant lifestyle. They express their pride in being narcos and most of them do not follow the tacit agreements established decades ago among the cartels and with the government. They do not hold the principle of giving back to their community as intrinsic. Neither have they maintained a low profile as did most of their predecessors. They are a new generation of kingpins who are less cautious about causing turf wars, and resort to more violence when conducting the business (Cervantes, 2018).
2 Various security forces in Mexico are included under the term "Mexican government." These are: federal and municipal police, the marines, the army, the AFI, PGR (Attorney General's office), SEDENA (Homeland Security), and the ministerial police.
3 Members of the Sinaloa cartel also have a presence on Facebook. For example, the Sinaloa cartel has a Facebook group dedicated to "El Chino Antrax" with more than 20,000 members. However, a larger fan based was found on Twitter. Also, while doing the content analysis, many tweets and Facebook posts were very similar and, for instance, repetitive pictures were upload. For this reason, in this case study Twitter was the social media platform used for the social network

analysis and to monitor the organization's social media usage. The content analysis was conducted in both Twitter and YouTube. It is worth noting something interesting about the cartel's Facebook pages, which is that during my preliminary research, most of the accounts I studied were open to the public. Going back to them a few months later, I found that most of these accounts had turned private. This limited my research on Facebook since some of the friend requests sent were never accepted.

4   In-degree centrality refers to the number of links or ties directed to a node. Betweenness centrality quantifies the number of times a node acts as a bridge between two or more other nodes (Freeman, 1977).
5   *El Blog del Narco* or *el Narco Blog* was created to report about the war on drugs in Mexico when the traditional media outlets were not doing so. It became extremely popular and was followed by millions of people.
6   Video originally available at: www.youtube.com/watch?v=eoKUtko4X6k (unavailable by the time of publication).
7   Available at: https://twitter.com/search?q=%40mzoficial&src=typd.
8   Tweet available at: https://twitter.com/search?q=%40mzoficial&src=typd (July 12, 2015).
9   Available at: https://twitter.com/search?q=%40mzoficial&src=typd (February 22, 2014).
10 In this model media censorship is considered an organizational shock since it was after the signing of the accord that their main platform of exposure, mainstream media, became unavailable for them. They later turned to social media.
11 According to the article, between 2013 and 2015, the Sinaloa cartel suffered 214 arrests, compared to 159 Gulf cartel members, 138 from CJNG, 136 Zetas, 130 from the Beltrán Leyva, 126 from La Familia Michoacana, 67 Caballeros Templarios, 48 from the Cartel Independiente de Acapulco, 13 from the Juárez cartel, and 5 from the Tijuana cartel. Report available at: www.eluniversal.com.mx/articulo/nacion/seguridad/2016/01/31/fuerzas-federales-pegan-la-estructura-del-cartel-de-sinaloa.

References

Beittel, J. S. (2013). *Mexico's drug trafficking organizations: Source and scope of the violence*. Congressional Research Service.

Cervantes, M. (2018). Quienes son los narco-juniors que lideran los carteles mexicanos? Grupo Formula, August 3. Retrieved from: www.radioformula.com.mx/noticias/20180803/iquest-quienes-son-los-narco-juniors-que-lideran-los-carteles-mexicanos/.

Congressional Research Service. (2019). *Mexico: Organized crime and drug Trafficking organizations*. CRS Report. Retrieved from: https://fas.org/sgp/crs/row/R41576.pdf.

Ellingwood, K. (2010). Mexican drug lord "Nacho" was quiet and ruthless. *Borderland Beat*. August 2. Retrieved from: www.borderlandbeat.com/2010/08/mexican-drug-lord-nacho-was-quiet-and.html.

Excélsior (2014, January 3). Holanda captura a aprendiz de Ismael El Mayo Zambada. *Excélsior*. Retrieved from: www.excelsior.com.mx/nacional/2014/03/12/948310.

Excélsior (2017). Dámaso López, "El Mini Lic," intentó matarnos: hijos de "El Chapo." Retrieved from: www.excelsior.com.mx/nacional/2017/02/08/1145177.

Freeman, L. (1977). A set of measures of centrality based upon betweenness. *Sociometry*, *40*(1), 35–41.

Felbad-Brown, V. (2013). *Despite its siren song, high-value targeting doesn't fit all: Matching interdiction patterns to specific narcoterrorism and organized-crime context*. Paper presented at the Counter Narco-Terrorism and Drug Interdiction Conference in Miami, September 16–19. Retrieved from: www.brookings.edu/wp-content/uploads/2016/06/FelbabBrown-Matching-Interdiction-Patterns-to-Specific-Threat-Environments.pdf.

Fox, E. (2012). Brother of Sinaloa kingpin extradited to U.S. InSight Crime. Retrieved from: www.insightcrime.org/news-briefs/brother-of-sinaloa-kingpin-extradited-to-us.

Grayson, G. W. (2014). *The Cartel: The story of Mexico's most dangerous criminal organizations and their impact on U.S. security*. Santa Barbara, CA: Praeger.

InSight Crime. (2016). Sinaloa Cartel Profile. InSight Crime. Retrieved from: www.insightcrime.org/mexico-organized-crime-news/knights-templar-profile/.

Janowitz, N. (2016). El legado de "El Chapo" pende de un hilo despues del secuestro de su hijo. VICE Mexico. Retrieved from: www.vice.com/es_latam/article/pa4nqg/legado-chapo-pende-hilo-despues-secuestro-hijo.

Johnson, N. F., Zhen, M., Vorobyeva, Y., Gabrield, A., Qi, H., Velasquez, N., Manrique, P., Johnson, D., Restrepo, E., Song, C., & Wuchty, S. (2016, June 17). New online ecology of adversarial aggregates: ISIS and beyond. *Science*, 352(6292), 1459–1463.

Keefe, P. R. (2012). Cocaine incorporated. *New York Times*. Retrieved from: www.nytimes.com/2012/06/17/magazine/how-a-mexican-drug-cartel-makes-its-billions.html?pagewanted=all.

Milenio (2014). "El Chino Antrax": su vida, su novia, su arresto. *Milenio*. Retrieved from: www.milenio.com/policia/Chino_Antrax-brazo-violento-del-cartel-de-Sinaloa-Jose_Rodrigo_Arechiga-Holanda_0_335366747.html.

Ramsey, G. (2012). Regional leader's death is blow to Sinaloa cartel: Officials. InSight Crime. Retrieved from: www.insightcrime.org/news-briefs/3362-regional-leaders-death-is-blow-to-sinaloa-cartel.

Woody, C. (2017). A major player in the struggle for control of the Sinaloa Cartel just surrendered in the US. Business Insider. Retrieved from: www.businessinsider.com/sinaloa-cartel-member-damaso-lopez-el-mini-lic-surrendered-to-the-us-2017-7.

Xiaonan, J., Machiraju, R., Ritter, A., & Yen, P. Y. (2015). *Examining the distribution, modularity, and community structure in article networks for systematic reviews*. AMIA Annual Symposium.

Chapter 4

The Zetas Cartel

The Zetas is a criminal organization that has transformed the drug trafficking business in Mexico. This is not only because of the group's diversification of criminal activities, but also because they introduced a new operational model and violence never seen before in any other Mexican drug cartel. The Zetas methodically violated many rules that traditional cartels,[1] such as the Sinaloa, Tijuana, and Beltrán Leyva, had followed for decades. The White House labeled the Zetas a "global menace," comparing them to criminal organizations of the caliber of the Camorra in Italy and the Yakuza in Japan (Grayson, 2014). The cartel developed a reputation for sadistic and savage acts, and they rapidly became associated with beheadings and public hyper-violence. After their split from the Gulf cartel in about 2010, the Zetas achieved the status of the second most powerful criminal group in Mexico, and the main challenger to the Sinaloa cartel's hegemony. By this time, the Zetas had expanded significantly, operating in 405 Mexican municipalities out of a total of 2,440 (161 more than the Gulf cartel), and the organization was 2.3 times larger than the Sinaloa cartel (Coscia & Rios, 2012). The areas where the Zetas operated, during the time of this study, show the highest numbers of drug-related homicides. According to Dudley and Rios (2013), in 2010, the municipalities with the Zetas' presence counted 10,169 drug-related homicides, compared to 6,388 in the areas of the Gulf cartel and 4,772 in the Tijuana cartel's domains. The Zetas also expanded their operations in Central America, collaborating with other gangs like the *Mara Salvatrucha*, or *MS-13*, in El Salvador and *los Kaibiles* in Guatemala, in an effort to control the shipments of cocaine along the Guatemala–Mexico corridors (Beittel, 2013).

This chapter investigates the Zetas cartel, starting with a brief account of their origins and current status in the first section. The second part of the chapter explores the cartel's survival capacity, revisiting their battles and the organization's response to organizational shocks. The third section studies the Zetas' presence on social media. I present a social network analysis of their Facebook accounts as well as an analysis of their Facebook and YouTube video content. The fourth part analyzes the relationship between social media usage and setbacks. The final section presents the closing remarks.

The Origins and Evolution of the Zetas: From Military Elites to *Sicarios*

The Zetas were born between 1996 and 1997. The group was created by Osiel Cárdenas Guillén, the main leader of the Gulf cartel at the time. The head of the cartel before Cárdenas Guillén was Juan García Abrego. The former capo brought the Gulf cartel to its glory days when he made a business pact with the Colombian Cali cartel to smuggle cocaine into the U.S., and created a meticulous system of money laundering through "*casas de cambio*," or money-exchange houses established in border cities, which allowed him to make cash deposits in Texas banks (Thorpe, 2013). García Abrego was captured on January 14, 1996 and charged with 22 counts of drug trafficking; he is serving 11 life sentences in a U.S. prison (Frontline, 2014).

Cárdenas Guillén took over after Abrego's arrest and quickly came to be amongst the most wanted drug traffickers in the world. He was also known as "*El Mata Amigos*" (Friend Killer) since he had betrayed and killed business partners who were also considered his friend. Stories tell that Cárdenas Guillén developed a cocaine addiction and suffered from anxiety and paranoia. He was obsessed with the idea that his rivals and allies were conspiring against him and planning his assassination. For this reason, he sought personal protection (Ravelo, 2013; Grayson & Logan, 2017). Cárdenas Guillén was looking for a strong and highly trained group able to operate sophisticated weaponry but, most importantly, with good insight into and information about their main rivals, the Attorney General's Office (PGR) and the Mexican army. Arturo Guzmán Decena, a military defector, also known as "El Z-1," was delegated by Cárdenas Guillén the responsibility to create such group. For this purpose, Guzmán Decena recruited 30 lieutenants who deserted from the Mexican army's Airborne Special Group Forces (Grupos Aeromóviles de Fuerzas Especiales, GAFES),[2] a specialized faction of the Mexican security forces. The group became the armed wing of the Gulf cartel and was named "the Zetas." The new recruits' training covered various capacities: they knew how to manage high-power weaponry and had expertise in communication surveillance and counterintelligence tactics (Ravelo, 2013). The Zetas provided the Gulf cartel with a competitive advantage over other criminal organizations (Grayson & Logan, 2017).

Osiel Cárdenas Guillén was arrested on March 17, 2003, in Matamoros, Tamaulipas by the Mexican army. After his capture, the Zetas were left without a fixed leadership or direction. Cárdenas Guillén's arrest left a vacuum that contending leaders from both the Gulf and the Zetas were trying to fill, fighting over the control of important drug corridors in cities like Matamoros, Reynosa, Tampico, Nuevo Laredo, Monterrey, Veracruz, and San Luis Potosí. By then, the Zetas' co-founder Arturo Decena Guzmán had died (2002), and the second in line to lead, Rogelio González Piñaza was detained in 2004. This marked the opportunity for Heriberto Lazcano "El Lazca" or "El Z-3" to take control (Beittel, 2013).

Under the leadership of Heriberto Lazcano Lazcano the Gulf cartel went through a restructuring process giving the Zetas more leverage within the cartel's operations. They were in charge of other lucrative criminal activities such as kidnappings for ransom, extortion, migrant smuggling, human trafficking, piracy, weapon smuggling, illegal mining, oil, natural gas, coal and gasoline theft (Correa-Cabrera, 2017), just to mention a few of their 24 criminal modalities. They established a broad financial umbrella and created an intrinsic network of bribes, coercion, and co-optation (Dudley & Rios, 2013). Soon after, the Zetas started to gain more power and influence.

The extradition to the U.S. of Cárdenas Guillén was finalized in 2007. He was charged with conspiracy to traffic large amounts of marijuana and cocaine, with violating the "drug kingpin statute,"[3] and also with threatening two DEA agents and one FBI officer in Tamaulipas in 1999 (CNN Mexico, 2011). Cárdenas Guillén shared important information with the American authorities, in exchange for a reduced sentence, which later had serious repercussions in the organization. After this, tensions between the Zetas and the Gulf started building and the cartel went through a stage of internal conflict culminating in their split in 2010 (Ravelo, 2013; Beittel, 2013). Once the Zetas started working as a cartel under the leadership of El Lazca, their expansion and power grew exponentially.

Lazcano died on October 7, 2012, and Miguel Angel Treviño "El Z-40," responsible for the *plaza* in the state of Nuevo León, took over the organization. Under his guidance, the Zetas continued successfully operating; nevertheless, hints of internal factionalizing started to appear. El Z-40 was arrested during the summer of 2013. His younger brother Omar Treviño "El Z-42" inherited the leadership of the Zetas. Omar Treviño's mandate was short; he was captured by the federal police on March 4, 2015 (Castillo, 2015).

Structure and Modus Operandi

The capture and extradition of Osiel Cárdenas Guillén in 2007 marks an important critical juncture in the evolution of the Zetas. Once Heriberto Lazcano Lazcano took control, he began a process of restructuring within the organization. The Zetas started operating under a *military-hierarchical* structure, and later, El Lazca rearranged the organization into a less centralized *franchise* configuration.[4] He created cells, appointing several lieutenants to control specific territories. For example, Miguel Treviño, before becoming the main leader, controlled the state of Nuevo León and Jorge Eduardo Costilla Sánchez "El Coss" managed the *plaza* in Matamoros, Tamaulipas. Others were responsible for the crossing points in border cities such as Nuevo Laredo and Reynosa. El Lazca also established cells in the southern states of Quintana Roo, Guerrero and Tabasco (Grayson & Logan 2017).

The Zetas' brutal and extremely violent business model differentiated them from traditional cartels, focusing on organized violence (Congressional Research Service, 2019). One of their characteristics is the practice of torture and beheadings, and the exposure of their victims' mutilated bodies in public spaces. This group was also the first to challenge established syndicates and attempt to take over their fixed territories. Under their expansionist strategy, they sought for domination and control of the main criminal activities carried out in specific territories (Coscia & Rios, 2012). Their tactics included market positioning and subletting. In other words, they extracted rent from already established criminal networks without the need to build their own infrastructure (Rios, 2012; Congressional Research Service, 2019).

The Zetas Today

According to Grayson (2014), since the death of Lazcano Lazcano in 2012, the Zetas have steadily declined from their peak between 2010 and 2012. As mentioned earlier, after the capture of Miguel Angel Treviño, his brother Omar Treviño took over the organization. Although he maintained the violent and sadistic ways of his brother, Omar Treviño had serious problems holding the organization together. After his capture in 2015, a new faction of the cartel arose: the *Cartel del Noreste* (CDN). The group worked as a cell under the Zetas' mandate, but they became independent and are principal enemies of what is now called the *Zetas Vieja Escuela* (Zetas Old School), which ironically condemns them for the level of operational cruelty. The Zetas have lost influence and power and have retreated from some territories. Nonetheless, the organization is still relevant in the drug trafficking arena in Mexico (Congressional Research Service, 2019).

The Zetas: Survival Capacity

The Zetas are no ordinary cartel. The vicious ways they go about their business have gained them hatred on many different fronts. For example, the Zetas are constantly targeted by the Mexican, the U.S., and the Guatemalan governments. Between 2010 and 2012 three drug cartels – Sinaloa, Beltrán Leyva, and the Gulf – and other groups allied to form the *Carteles Unidos* (CU), to combat and eradicate the Zetas (*La Verdad*, 2019). The Cartel Jalisco Nueva Generación created a group called *los Matazetas* (the Zeta's killers), with presence mainly in the state of Veracruz. As their name implies, their sole mission was to banish this group and "clean Mexico from these dregs of society," as they state in their introductory video on YouTube.[5] Ironically, the Zetas have now joined CU to combat CJNG (*La Verdad*, 2019).

The rise of neo or non-traditional criminal organizations has restructured the dynamics of drug trafficking in Mexico. When the Zetas revealed their new business model, the Mexican security forces and rival cartels were not enough to contain the damage the criminal group was causing. In many towns in Tamaulipas the abuses of the Zetas became intolerable for the residents so they also started fighting them. Civilians created self-defense groups and with this the Zetas gained a new enemy. These groups formed in rural areas, usually ungoverned spaces that have become nests for drug cartels. Although the government denies their existence, in Tamaulipas two self-defense groups or community police groups were established. One originated in San Fernando, a municipality that has witnessed the massacre of thousands of migrants mostly from Central America. The other, called "Columna Pedro Méndez," was formed in the communities of Hidalgo, Mainero, and Villagrán (González, 2016). Another tactic the civilians are using is to denounce the cartel on social media. I further elaborate on this in the following section.

The Zetas have suffered significant disruptions to their organization. Their *modus operandi* has attracted more enemies than allies. If this organization is facing attacks from more actors than any other cartel in Mexico, how have the Zetas been able to achieve so much expansion and growth? What explains the Zetas' survival capacity? Experts have put several hypotheses forward. One argument attributes the Zetas' expansion to their military formation, since they were trained with cutting-edge warfare techniques, military strategy, and mastery of the use of weapons. This gave them a competitive advantage over the other cartels. However, this argument has lost credibility since all of the 14 original founders, the ones highly trained, are long gone from the organization; they are either dead or in prison (Beittel, 2013). Other explanations for their success refer to their ability to incite terror, their novel business model, and the decentralized structure adopted later. The Zetas have served as a model that newer criminal organizations such as La Familia Michoacana try to imitate without enjoying the same success.

Despite all the enemies they confront, the Zetas managed to survive, and expanded more than any other group in a relatively short period of time. Following the same process as the previous case study, I analyze the Zetas through assessing their battles and their reactions to major organizational disruptions.

The Battles

Graph 4.1 presents the reported clashes the Zetas cartel faced from 2006 to 2015. Taking into account that from 2006 to 2010 the Zetas worked for the Gulf cartel, the battles chosen to include in the data are those attributed specifically to the group of hired assassins. *El Universal*'s archives included 7,180 reports related to the Zetas during the scope of this study. The analysis presented here is based on 721 of the notes that met the criteria.

The data shows that most of the battles reported involved the Zetas versus the Mexican government, accounting for 72 percent of the counted clashes. During the war years, different governmental security forces have

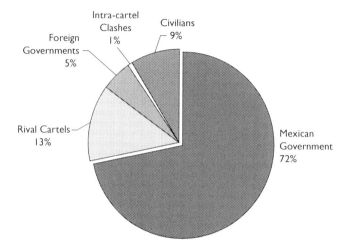

Graph 4.1 The Zetas' Reported Clashes 2006–2015.

been involved in these battles. For example, from 2007, when the Zetas started carrying bigger responsibilities in the Gulf cartel's operations, their main enemy was the Mexican army. The following year, the governmental security body they fought the most was the federal police. From 2010 to 2012 the cartel was mostly targeted by the army once again. By 2014, their worst enemy became the *Grupo de Armas y Tácticas Especiales* (GATES).

Confrontations with rival cartels account for 13 percent, which seems a low share considering that they had more enemies, at the time, than other drug cartels in Mexico. It is important to remember that in states such as Tamaulipas and Veracruz, in which this criminal group widely operates, confrontations involving the cartels were rarely reported, so there is a possibility that this figure is somewhat higher. The cartel has also faced pursuit from foreign governments, which accounts for 5 percent of their battles. The foreign governments that target this organization are mainly the U.S. and Guatemala. Thus, three governments in Central America – Guatemala, Honduras, and El Salvador – founded the *Fuerzas Combinates' Especiales* (Combined Special Forces) security group, to battle the Zetas, not mainly because of the drug dealing problem, but because they have been held responsible for the vanishing of thousands of migrants from those countries who travel through Mexico to get to the U.S. Just in a period of six months during 2009, 9,758 migrants were kidnapped, presumably by the Zetas. There are estimates of 70,000 migrants misplaced as of 2016 (Guzmán, 2016). Nonetheless, compared to the Sinaloa cartel, the Zetas deal with far fewer attacks by foreign governments.

What is especially interesting about the data gathered here is that nine percent of clashes reported have been with civilians, adding a new enemy to the cartel's list of enemies. The Zetas have been responsible for attacks in public areas where dozens of innocent people have died. One scandalous case was the bombing in 2011 of the Casino Royal in Monterrey, Nuevo León, which resulted in the death of 52 civilians. Another occurrence was the bombing in 2008 in Morelia's historic center during a commemoration on the Mexican Independence Day, with four casualties and many people injured. As mentioned earlier, the Zetas have orchestrated the kidnapping and murder of thousands of migrants. Hundreds of bodies have been discovered in countless clandestine graves with the bodies of people mainly from Central America, as in the gruesome case of 70 massacred immigrants found in San Fernando, Tamaulipas. One of the bloodiest, but least known, massacres authored by the Zetas took place in Allende, Coahuila, close to Piedras Negras, a border town that became an important transshipment point for smuggling controlled by the Zetas. There are estimates that about 300 people were killed and their bodies burned. The reason behind the attack was that the Treviño Morales brothers, Miguel Angel (Z-40) and Omar (Z-42) Treviño believed that three people working for them were collaborating with the U.S. authorities and had committed treason. As a form of retaliation, the Zetas occupied two towns over a weekend full of horrors. The collusion of the local authorities with the cartel was undeniable since none of the 20 officials on duty patrolled the cities or assisted them in any of the attacks. These are small towns and the shooting or the kidnapping and later killing of close to 300 people would be noticeable (Paullier, 2016). All of these despicable situations have caused resentment from society towards the criminal organization. Certainly, in Mexico, drug trafficking–related violence is not uncommon, but the Zetas brought it to another level. Traditionally, drug cartels did not interfere with the lives of the average civilian; the Zetas changed this dynamic, so much so that civilian conflicts show up as a noteworthy share of the reported battles. In the face of the cartel's apparent impunity, the population have responded to the Zetas attacks in various ways. The interaction between the Zetas and civil society takes an interesting turn when social media is added into the equation.

The Zetas have a broader list of enemies to fight against compared to other criminal groups such as the Sinaloa cartel, but, then again, they have managed to survive. The next section examines the way in which the Zetas have responded to organizational setbacks.

Organizational Disruptions and the Zetas Response

Some of the most important disruptions that the Zetas have experienced took place when they were still part of the Gulf cartel; nevertheless, such disturbances also affected the Zetas directly since the group worked with a degree of autonomy. This list of crucial organizational shocks encompasses probably some of the most vicious and violent individuals that have ever run a drug trafficking organization in Mexico, capable of crimes from torturing, dismembering, and making puree out of their victims, dissolving them in acid, to eating them.

Several of the Zetas' leaders did not witness the split from the Gulf cartel. This is the case with Jaime González "El Hummer." He is one of the original founders of the armed group that deserted from the Mexican military in 1999 to join the Zetas. He has been recorded as a bloodthirsty leader (Hernandez Herrera, 2014). El Hummer served as a *sicario* for nine years under the mandate of Heriberto Lazcano Lazcano. Their closeness opened the path for El Hummer to become head of the *plaza* in Reynosa, Tamaulipas. His domains included five key municipalities, among them his native San Luis Potosí. He was captured by the federal police on November 7, 2008 and admitted to the maximum-security penitentiary of *El Altiplano* in Almoloya de Juárez in the state of Mexico, sentenced to 35 years (Hernandez Herrera, 2014).

According to Grayson (2014), the Zetas suffered another significant blow with the capture of Raúl Lucio Hernández Lechuga "El Lucky." Founder and leader of the cartel, he made the list of the 37 most wanted criminals in Mexico and was of high interest to the DEA (SEMAR, 2011). He was responsible for the cartel's criminal activities in ten states across the country including: Hidalgo, Oaxaca, Puebla, Veracruz, Tabasco, Campeche, Querétaro, San Luis Potosí, Quintana Roo, and Mexico. The Mexican marines arrested El Lucky on December 12, 2011 in a ranch in Veracruz during his own birthday celebration.

The organization also experienced an important setback with the arrest of Flavio Méndez Santiago "El Amarillo," another original founder of the Zetas, in mid-January 2011, in the state of Oaxaca. He also made the list of the 37 most wanted criminals in the country. Méndez was recruited in 1993 and later became the leader of the cartel's *halcones*[6] (hawks) in the northern states of Nuevo León and Tamaulipas. Later, he was responsible for the operations in southern Mexico, and was in charge of one of the most lucrative illicit activities of the cartel, controlling the flow of illegal immigrants coming from Central and South America (InSight Crime, 2016b).

Later in 2012, the organization suffered two key shocks. On September 26, Iván Velázquez Caballero "El Talibán" was captured by the Mexican marines. This important figure in the organization was the appointed regional leader of the cartel at one of the most important crossing points, Nuevo Laredo, Tamaulipas. In 2007, he was relocated to the state of Zacatecas. From there, he ascended to the top echelons of the Zetas, becoming a key financial operator and money launderer for the cartel. By 2012, he was serving as a top commander in several states across the Mexican territory. The arrest of El Talibán is thought to have been a set up. According to some reports, before his capture, El Talibán was planning on turning against other top leaders of the organization (Pachico, 2012). He was becoming a dangerous individual for the drug cartel.

Just a few days later, on October 7, the marines confronted the Zetas on a rural road in upstate Coahuila, near Progreso. Later it became known that one of the narcos killed during the shooting was the one and only Heriberto Lazcano Lazcano, the top leader of the organization at the time. Lazcano was also known as the "Z-3," or "The Executioner," the latter a nickname earned due to his aggressive and ruthless ways of conducting the business. He is considered one of the most merciless leaders of the Zetas. El Lazca became like a spiritual leader for the organization, and recruits really respected him and felt pride working for him. He created a sense of fraternity among the Zetas. Under his guidance, the cartel seemed at its strongest, demonstrating a great degree of unity and stability.

After Lazcano's death, Miguel Angel Treviño Morales, alias "Z-40," rose to power. Although his mandate did not last long (less than a year), he left his mark. He had been responsible for the *plaza* in Nuevo Laredo for a long time. Later, in 2007, he had gone to Veracruz to replace a high-ranking leader after his death. He then controlled the drug trafficking in that corridor. Treviño also took over the DVD and CD piracy business, and human trafficking. The capture of this capo was one of the most important victories of Peña Nieto's administration.

The natural successor of Miguel Angel was his brother, Omar Treviño Morales the "Z-42." Like his brother, Omar Treviño had a long history of working for the Zetas. He continued the tradition of brutal violence. He has been recorded as the man responsible for the mass killings in San Fernando. His participation in criminal activities includes extortions, kidnappings, and drug trafficking. The DEA offered a $5 million reward in exchange for information leading to his capture (InSight Crime, 2016a). Omar was captured during the early hours of March 5, 2015 in a high-end residence in the municipality of San Pedro Garza Garcia in Monterrey, Mexico, one of the richest neighborhoods in Latin America (Pérez Salazar, 2015). He was considered a strong leader, but by the time he took charge, the organization was having internal issues, and the split was foreseeable.

After reviewing the most significant organizational setbacks the Zetas underwent until 2015, Figure 4.1 reflects how the organization has reacted towards them, showing alterations or readjustments in their criminal activities before and after these shocks.

Figure 4.1 shows that the indicators of violence and criminal activities start rising months after the extradition of Osiel Cárdenas Guillén in 2007. Before this time, in 2006 and part of 2007, the figures remain relatively lower compared to the following years. As mentioned earlier, after the extradition of the leader to the U.S. in 2007 the Gulf cartel went through a restructuration process in which the Zetas were given more power and

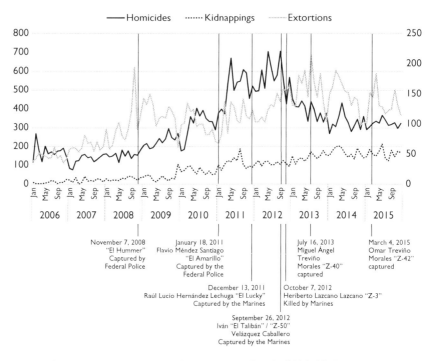

Figure 4.1 The Zetas' Response to Organizational Shocks 2006–2015.

tensions started building up internally. The increase of violence and criminal activities during this time is reflected in the model. In the following years, the Zetas' criminal activities reveal some spikes, especially in the number of homicides between 2011 and 2012, and after the loss of two important leaders, "El Amarillo" and later "El Lucky." To put it in context, during those years the organization had not completed its split from the Gulf cartel. In addition, it was during this time that the Zetas reached their highest level of growth and expansion throughout the Mexican territory. This was a period of intra-cartel disturbances as well as intense confrontations against other organizations, now also including the Gulf cartel. The rate of homicides reached its highest point between El Lucky's capture and the arrest of El Talibán on September 2012. After this, the rate of violence decreased almost by half and stayed like that even after the death of Heriberto Lazcano Lazcano.

The death of El Lazca was not expected to have the same kind of operational impact that it would have had several years earlier. This is also reflected in the model presented above. After his capture, probably one of the most vital setbacks for the Zetas, the indicators of presence do not seem to change much with the exception of extortions, reaching the highest level after his death. Dudley and Rios (2013) state that after the passing of the bloody leader, the cartel faced division and disorder. Although indicators of violence appear to be lower, indicators of criminal activities, especially extortions, spiked during the power transition between El Lazca and Miguel Angel Treviño, remaining high until the end of this study.

It might be the transition from a military-hierarchical to a more decentralized structure that made the organization more resistant to significant organizational shocks, so that the cartel does not appear to destabilize meaningfully at least up to 2015. According to experts, decentralized structures make an organization more resilient to important setbacks. In addition, theory states that when top leaders of criminal organizations are taken down, violence tends to go up. In the case of the Zetas, the trend does not appear to apply after decentralization, since leaders had become simply agents who could be quickly substituted or supplanted. This variable might help to explain why the indicators of violence and criminal activities through the war years, for this criminal group, have remained relatively steady. Finally, the cartel appears to be in constant turmoil, having transitory or short-term leaderships, and this might again be due to the highly decentralized nature they eventually adopted. This structural arrangement has resulted in higher elasticity when major setbacks befall, solidifying their survival capacity. However, constant internal commotion can, in the long run, fracture the organization, as happened to the Zetas later. This is not reflected in Figure 4.1 since the split of the Zetas and the Cartel del Noreste happened in 2016 (Proceso, 2016), a year beyond the scope of this study.

The Zetas Cartel's Usage of Social Media

Like the Sinaloa cartel, the Zetas have also taken advantage of technology and social media platforms. The Zetas got the international spotlight when relevant international journals such as The *New York Times*, The *Washington Post*, and academic outlets such as the *Yale Journal of International Affairs*, followed up an unprecedented incident that has been called the "cyber war of Anonymous vs. the Zetas." The conflict consisted of an interchange of threats mainly via social media platforms between the two groups. A series of YouTube videos were uploaded by the hacktivists, in which they threatened the cartel with dissemination of critical information about their physical operational network if they did not comply with demands for the liberation of three members of Anonymous, kidnapped during a demonstration in the state capital of Veracruz. The first of several videos was posted on October 6, 2011; it lasts two and a half minutes and has had 661,537 views. In this particular video, a representative of Anonymous, dressed in their characteristic attire (Guy Fawkes or Vendetta mask and a black suit), also explains to the marines and the Mexican army their discomfort and enragement with the crimes committed by the Zetas, especially against innocent people, and with the impunity they enjoy for their crimes.[7] What makes this case unique is that never before had a group of civilians so openly and successfully threatened a powerful drug cartel in Mexico. This case is discussed again later in this chapter.

The context in which social media usage functions within the Zetas' domains has unfolded differently from the setting in which the Sinaloa cartel operates. In their areas, especially in Tamaulipas and Veracruz, traditional media has been highly censored and social media platforms took over as an alternative outlet of information. The unfoldings of the virtual interactions between the Zetas, the authorities, and the citizenry, have created an unprecedented situation, altering in some ways the dynamics of the drug war.

This section follows the path set out in the preceding chapters. I performed a social network analysis in order to illustrate the cartel's online presence. In this case, I conducted the analysis on Facebook. In contrast to the Sinaloa cartel members, it appears that Facebook is the preferred social platform for the Zetas members. After investigating their Twitter accounts, I found that their use of this outlet is limited and mostly systematic. Many alleged Zetas members' Twitter accounts are short-lived; in other words, the accounts they open last just a few weeks and serve a specific purpose. For instance, many of the posts are menacing messages tagging a specific person. Image 4.1 is an example of these posts.

In Image 4.1, the tweet reads, "@MVeronica you are the next one to die." This particular account contains only three messages, all of them in reference to killing Veronica.[8] It was active just for a few days. Again, these types of publications and the short life span of their accounts are apparently a common practice of the Zetas on Twitter. For this reason, it was not possible to build a reliable representation of their network on this platform, or conduct a proper analysis of its usage and content. It was, however, feasible to do it for their Facebook accounts. Figure 4.2 is a depiction of the Zetas cartel's Facebook network.

Directing a social network analysis on this platform was more challenging than doing it for Twitter since NodeXL does not have the legal rights or authorization to download information on an individual's network of friends from Facebook accounts. In order to construct the database for the

Image 4.1

Source: https://twitter.com/loszetasoficial.

analysis, I examined personal accounts one by one, linking each individual node and edges manually through their friends in common until a network was unveiled and, next, I used centrality measures to find the most important nodes in the network. This simplified version of the cartel's Facebook network (Figure 4.2) presents a total of 142 nodes with a fan base of approximately 40,000 friends and followers.

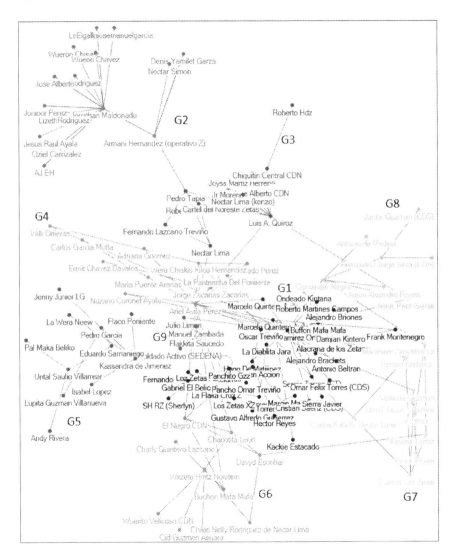

Figure 4.2 The Zetas' Facebook Network.

Source: Created with NodeXL Pro (http://nodexl.codeplex.com) from the Social Media Research Foundation (www.smrfoundation.org)

The Zetas' Facebook network exhibits a complex decentralized structure. The illustration shows that their level of decentralization gives roots for additional subnetworks to emerge, mimicking their composition at the physical level. This network divides into various clusters forming nine main groups, each one offering different pieces of information about the cartel. For instance, Group 9 (G9) and Group 8 (G8) tell us that members of rival cartels and affiliates of Mexican security forces closely monitor their enemies through their social media profiles. In this case, Junior Guzman, a leader of the Sinaloa cartel and a central node in their network, Manuel Zambada, and Jorge Silva from the same illicit group have befriended a couple of members of the Zetas, such as Jesus Alejandro Reyes and Antonio de Medina. Likewise, a member of SEDENA (Secretariat of National Defense) under the name of *Soldado Activo* (Active Soldier) is Facebook friends with Julio Limon and Flakkita Saucedo, persons with a significant degree of centrality in the Zetas' Facebook network. Facebook is different from Twitter in the sense that, in the first instance, an approved request is necessary in order to be registered as friends and have reciprocal access to someone's information; also, it depends on the privacy settings on each individual account. In other words, all parties here are aware of the access of rival groups to their information and the fact that they are interested in monitoring their accounts. The purpose of this could be strategic, or to maintain intelligence on each other.

Groups 7 and 6 (G7, G6) represent the newest faction of the organization, and presently one of their worst enemies, the Cartel del Noreste (CDN); many of these profiles were created in 2015. In these accounts, it can be seen how some Zetas changed their Facebook status from "working for the Zetas" or "the Company" to "working for CDN." Through their posts, the imminent rupture of the cartel can be perceived. Group 5 (G5) and Group 3 (G3) reflect a juxtaposition of the cells formed by members of the Zetas Old School, Nectar Lima, and CDN. The next group, Group 4 (G4), corresponds mainly to accounts from first generation Zetas. Also in these groups, the organization's factions from other countries are detectable; there are Zetas from Bolivia, Peru, and the U.S., especially some with geolocation in the state of Texas. In this group, the node with the highest degree of betweenness is Ariel Avila Perez, leader of the Zetas in Bolivia, who was later transferred to Nuevo Laredo, Tamaulipas. Group 2 (G2) represents the Nectar Lima division of the cartel and Group 1 (G1) is a hub with rival cartels' accounts. These profiles have links to "Alacrana de los Zetas" and to Marcelo Quintero Avila, whose accounts have an important degree of centrality. Several members of the Sinaloa cartel, the Caballeros Templarios, and the Gulf cartel are part of this module of the network.

The network does not present strong central figures, but there are a couple of nodes with high centrality. Notably, and inversely from the previous case study, the main capos of the Zetas, such as El Lazca, Miguel Angel

Treviño, "El Hummer," or Omar Treviño, do not have Facebook or Twitter accounts or proxies. I found some accounts under their names, but they specified they are just parodies. The rest of the accounts do not have reliable content and do not follow the criteria for veracity used in this work.

The social media presence of the Zetas is not as prominent as the Sinaloa cartel. Unlike Twitter, Facebook allows a limit of 5,000 friends per account. In addition, it is possible, as in Twitter, to "follow" accounts; nonetheless, the number of followers on the accounts studied here does not compare to the Twitter followers base of the Sinaloa cartel. Still, the Zetas have thousands of followers. In this network, the entire universe is composed of more than 47,000 nodes. They do have strong presence on YouTube with about 196,000 videos related to the cartel. The subject matter of the Zetas' accounts is evaluated in the next section.

Facebook and YouTube Content Analysis

In Chapter 3, terms such as *gruesome* and *vile* were used to describe the content on the accounts of the Sinaloa cartel members. Clearly, I was clueless and unprepared for the current case study. The Zetas have made decapitations their trademark to get terrible crimes attributed to them in order to spread terror. At one point in this study, decapitation seemed a mild practice compared to what I found as the investigation progressed.

I encountered some similarities between the Sinaloa's and the Zetas' social media content. Yet, some important differences stand out. This section reflects on the content and purpose of Facebook and YouTube usage by the Zetas.

Facebook Content Analysis

The Zetas' Facebook accounts' content, among other things, reveals details about demographic characteristics of the members of the organization. In particular, the Zetas include more women on their workforce compared to the Sinaloa cartel. Furthermore, they recruit teenagers as young as 13 years old, both boys and girls, who are trained as soldiers, *sicarios*, or hawks. It seems as if a military background is no longer required for the new recruits. This gives an idea of how low the barriers of entry to the organization have become.

The Zetas' economic position and level of education are evident. In most of the accounts studied, it is apparent that, compared to the members of the Sinaloa cartel, their narco-life is less glamorous. They do proudly show their new trucks or cars, but they are less luxurious or extravagant than those of their rivals. Their writing skills and spelling on their posts show a low literacy level. What is more, it is noticeable that a good proportion of their members are English speakers. Some of their accounts have posts written in Spanglish,[9] which is a common practice for the inhabitants of the U.S.–Mexico border area in which this cartel has important headquarters. This sheds light on the fact that some recruits of the Zetas come from the U.S. side of the border. In some cases, the mass deportations of immigrants from the U.S. to the Mexican border has given the cartel the opportunity to recruit new members, many times by resorting to forced recruitment. Having English speaking collaborators eases the process of conducting business in the northern country. The results of the content analysis from Facebook are summarized in Graph 4.2.

Similar to the Sinaloa cartel, a high percentage of the Zetas' content on Facebook is related to posting pictures and descriptions about their operations and combats: 35 percent of their posts contain images of them ready to embark on a mission, videos of live shootings, and images of the aftermath of the battles. The visuals entail bodies massacred by bullets, the interior of their vehicles stained with blood and burned out from the flames of grenades used during a confrontation.

The second main purpose of using Facebook (17 percent) is to praise their organization and its leaders. The Zetas show a lot of pride in being part of the cartel. They often post pictures of themselves in their uniforms and caps with the logo of the "company," as they call it sometimes. The next set of posts consist of pictures of the weapons they use, which are not as sophisticated as the ones the members of the Sinaloa cartel show; they do not show gold-plated or diamond-studded pistols or rifles. In addition, they post images of piles of money and bulk cargoes of drugs they traffic which, with the weaponry, accounts for 12 percent of the content. Next on the list, with 11 percent, are videos. Some of these videos are to honor cartel members lost in battles, but most of them are *narcoraps*. *Narcoraps* are similar to *narcocorridos*. In these songs, they describe epic adventures, send messages to rivals, and talk about what makes their cartel great and strong, honoring

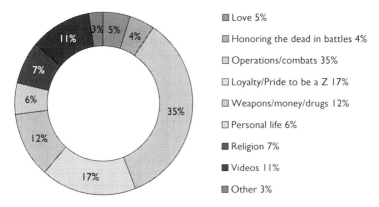

Graph 4.2 The Zetas' Facebook Content Analysis.

their leaders as legendary heroes. It is possible that since the Zetas recruit people from Texan border cities, mainly from Laredo to Brownsville, they have more exposure and influence to rap and hip-hop music.

Another category found in the content is religion (7 percent). The Zetas' main Catholic saint is San Judas Tadeo. It can be considered a case of syncretism[10] since they also pray to the Holy Death. They post picture collages portraying San Judas Tadeo holding an AR-15 rifle with the Holy Death in the background. The narcoculture has become embedded in Mexico during the last decade. On the religious side, hints of *Santeria* and Catholic practices are mixed. The purpose of posting these images is to pray for their lives and for protection during battles and missions.

One more sort of posts from members of this group includes those about their personal life (6 percent). This is a type of content that was not found as much in the previous case. These type of publications have pictures of friends, family, and their ordinary life. On these posts, Zetas members seem like regular people. It is hard to believe sometimes that the *sicarios* and *sicarias* are moms and dads, daughters and sons, brothers and sisters. Four of the accounts followed in this study were from women. Two of them were reported killed by family members or friends posting on their walls to honor their lives. The remaining categories in the content analysis are posts about love (5 percent), honoring Zetas that have been killed during battles (4 percent), and lastly other type of content (3 percent).

YouTube Content Analysis

Overall, the content of the videos the Zetas upload to YouTube and the details former members describe in video interviews on how the cartel works are hard to conceive, digest, believe, reason, and they are sources of true nightmares. The subject matter of their videos demonstrates their monopoly of terror.

Graph 4.3 shows the shares of the content the Zetas broadcast on YouTube. Most of the videos found (23 percent) are clips from different state or national news outlets related to the cartel, showing the "last letter," or reporting the capture or death of a top leader, a dismantled cell, confiscated weapons and drugs, and notes about their gruesome crimes. Next in quantity are threatening messages totaling 18 percent of the content. The Zetas are very successful at getting their menacing messages across on this platform. The footage displayed here is hard to watch. The videos show, for example, one or more captured members of rival cartels on their knees with Zetas behind them holding long-barreled weapons pointing at them; in the meantime someone is shouting questions and being filmed. This is the interrogation strategy used by the Zetas to make members of opponent organizations confess or give out information about their location, plans, missions, or leaders. The point of these videos is to make clear the consequences that anyone interfering with the Zetas will suffer. The sigh of terror

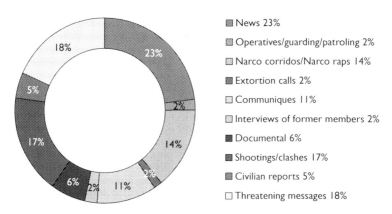

Graph 4.3 The Zetas' YouTube Content Analysis.

in the eyes of the prisoners confessing, knowing they will die at any second, is truly chilling. Some of the videos are censored, though complete versions can be found on web pages such as *Blog del Narco*, but some videos play the complete footage with someone getting tortured, shot, or slowly beheaded.

The next category consists of videos about shootings and clashes with 17 percent of the content. Here, live battles and their aftermath are publicized. Following this are *narcoraps* clips with 14 percent, and then communiques with 11 percent of the content. These reports contain information about the status of the cartel and future plans; for instance, they announce in which cities they will be fighting for turf, warning the citizenry not to leave their homes late at night during those days. Documentaries about the cartel, most of them in English, make up 6 percent of the content. Some of these documentaries contain interviews with former or current cartel members in which they reveal in great detail how it is to be a Zeta. They tell stories about their recruitment process and the way they practice discipline. In the interviews, current and former members describe the punishments they face, the same for men and women. A recurring technique is one call *"tablazos."* The reprimand consists of being hit by a piece of wood, specially tailored with very specific characteristics. The stick of wood, as they describe it, has specific measurements and has three holes in the middle in order to break the air to hit harder, leaving deep scars on their bodies. The Zetas apply this method to all members that make some type of mistake while working, such as omitting to report a police car. The stories get darker when they talk about how they take care of the bodies of all the people they kill, from dissolving them in barrels full of acid, to making stew out of them. The rest of the videos are civilians reporting of the cartel operations or whereabouts with 5 percent, followed by isolated interviews with former members, clips of operations, and extortion calls recorded by the victims each with 2 percent.

The Changing Dynamics of the Drug War: A War of All against All

A drug war is usually fought between the government or state security forces and drug cartels, so threats flowing between these agents are expected. Yet, based on the data gathered from the content analysis of YouTube, an undercurrent of changing aspects of the war can be perceived. In the "threats" category analyzed in the previous section, the exchange of messages does not only happen between the usual actors (the government or rival drug cartels), but the hostile interactions include civilians as well.

The shares of these threats are displayed in Graph 4.4. The data shows that just 5 percent of the hostile messages occur between the Zetas and the government. A great part, 78 percent, of the threats presented in the YouTube content are between the Zetas and other rival cartels. The Zetas receive 48 percent of the menacing messages from rival groups and the Zetas are responsible for 30 percent of the generated messages. Then, civilians come into the picture. Of the civilian threats that are posted in YouTube videos (17 percent altogether), 10 percent are targeted from the Zetas to citizens and 7 percent are threats from civilians against the cartel.

Civilians became active participants in the drug war, adding yet another enemy fighting against the Zetas. As briefly discussed earlier in this chapter, for citizens in states such as Tamaulipas and Veracruz, in which traditional media has been harshly censored and impunity is high, social media became a source of information. And with anonymity playing a central role, civilians use social media also as an instrument and platform to report on the cartels and the injustices they themselves are suffering. Yet, this has provoked not

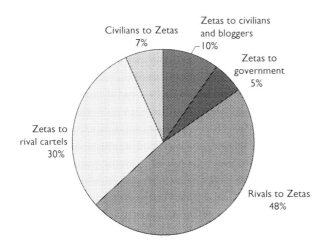

Graph 4.4 The Zetas' Share of Threats.

only retaliation from the Zetas towards civilians reporting on them, but also prosecution from the government.

With the rise in the use of web-based social platforms, the control of information became difficult for the government and the cartels to regulate. They took some measures. On the one hand, in addition to the violations of human rights from the military that civilians have witnessed since the war started (Human Rights Watch, 2016), they have also faced retribution from the authorities for reporting drug war–related issues on social media. Some state governments have made the reporting by civilians of drug-related issues on these platforms a crime. In the state of Veracruz, for example, reporting on a shooting or a blockade on social media that is not proven accurate is now considered a misdemeanor under the charges of "terrorism and sabotage," which under the Mexican law can result in a 30-year sentence (Soberanes, 2011).

On the other hand, the cartels are also trying to dissuade civilians from reporting by using extreme violence. Not only has Mexico become one of the most dangerous countries for journalists killed by cartels, but the Zetas have also started killing cyber activists and bloggers who were trying to fill out the informational vacuum left by traditional media when it comes to reporting on the drug war. There are some notorious occurrences demonstrating these dynamics of the war. One example is the case of the murder by the Zetas of Maria Elizabeth Macías, who reported under the pseudonym "NenaDLaredo" on the social networking site *Nuevo Laredo en Vivo*. In this portal, heated interchanges about the drug war took place, and real-time information about cartel clashes in the city was constantly reported. Her page urged people to report on cartels' and the military's whereabouts for the sake of their own survival. Two weeks later, in the same city, the bodies of two young men were found hanging from a bridge with another note,[11] again signed by the Zetas, mentioning and menacing the authors and participants of three web sites and blogs, including the most popular *Blog del Narco*, demanding they stop the reporting. Later, in Reynosa, Tamaulipas, on October 17, 2014, Twitter exploded with feeds of the assassination of Doctor Maria del Rosario Fuentes Rubio, collaborator on the page *Valor por Tamaulipas* that served as another platform of civil journalism. The doctor was reported missing for a few days until a series of messages were posted on her Twitter page. In the first post from her Twitter page the doctor states: "Friends and family, my real name is Maria del Rosario Fuentes Rubio, I am a doctor and today my life has come to an end." In the second post she warns Twitter users not to make the same mistake as she did (reporting on cartels), "nothing is gained from it, on the contrary, today I realize that I found death with nothing in return," and she continues, "they are closer than you think." In her last post she advises Twitter users who report on *Valor por Tamaulipas* pages to close their accounts, "do not put your families at risk, like I did, I plead for their forgiveness."[12] Finally, the last post includes a picture of her lifeless body. The authors of the homicide were never prosecuted, found, or convicted, which adds to the frustration and indignation of the population. Despite the cartels' dreadful attempt to stop the flow of information via social media, people continue to report on them until this day. Some others have faced the same fate as the cases just mentioned.

Another less tragic example in which a group of civilians threatened the Zetas was the previously mentioned episode, the so-called "cyber war" between the Zetas and the hacktivist group Anonymous. In brief, members of Anonymous publicly demanded of the Zetas, through social media, the liberation of three of their members kidnapped during a demonstration in the capital of Veracruz, the incident taking place back in October 2011. The hashtag #*OpCartel* (created specially to get mass exposure on the issue) and the particulars of this asymmetrical interaction got the attention of news outlets around the world.

One last example to illustrate how complex the interaction between actors in the drug war has become is that of the time when the citizens, the cartels, and the government joined forces to fight a common enemy, the Zetas, in the midst of chaos. Three main drug cartels in Mexico, Carteles Unidos under the lead of the Sinaloa cartel, got together to get rid of the Zetas (Vega, 2011). This strange occurrence took place sometime around the autumn of 2011. Although there are no official records from the government, during my investigation of the Sinaloa cartel's social media content, I found it stated on the Twitter account presumably owned by El Mayo that the government had asked the cartel to aid them in their fight against the Zetas. During this time, through *narcomantas* and social media, the Sinaloa cartel urged the citizenship in Tamaulipas, Veracruz, Zacatecas, and Nuevo León to report on the Zetas in order that they could find them. Citizens responded to the request. They posted on Facebook and Twitter pages tagging members of the Sinaloa cartel, informing them of houses used by the Zetas to keep kidnapped people, drugs, or weaponry. They informed about small stores and places they operated, and even reported on places members of the Zetas gathered or lived.

Social Media and Organizational Shocks

The main puzzle of this book revolves around the question of whether or not the use of social media by the Mexican drug cartels has any influence on their survival capacity. As in the Sinaloa case, the media censorship in Mexico in 2011 is included in the model. The latter is considered a significant organizational shock in this case, since exposure on mainstream media became unavailable for the Zetas as a means to spread messages. Figure 4.3 shows the online behavior on Facebook before and after each key organizational setback.

I expected to see no social media (Facebook) activity from 2006 to mid-2011, since its use in Mexico only gathered momentum around 2010, and the adoption process took some time. Then, between 2012 and 2013 the

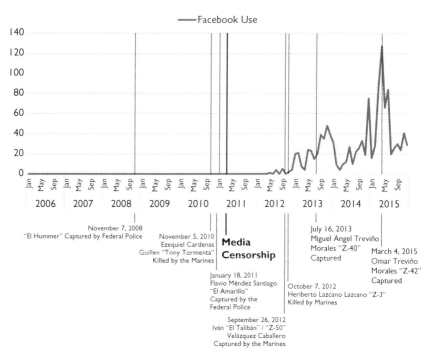

Figure 4.3 The Zetas' Facebook Usage and Organizational Shocks 2006–2015.

use of Facebook by members of the Zetas rises significantly. The data suggests that by 2013, the Zetas had to a great extent adopted social media for their communication strategies. It is not until 2015 that their Facebook activity reaches its highest point, particularly at the time of the arrest of Omar Treviño. The SNA I have performed points to fragmentations and the formation of a new faction that later became the Cartel del Noreste and the actual principal enemy of the Zetas. This suggests that during the leadership of Omar Treviño there was already some internal fracturing of the cartel. The turbulent period is reflected in the activity of the Zetas Facebook accounts when some of them started to transition to the CDN. It is important to take into consideration that the thriving Facebook presence may be due to the recruitment of young soldiers, some of them still teens, which is a generation that tends to rely significantly on social media.

The Analysis

The Zetas adopted social media into their communication strategies for running psychological warfare. Following the hypotheses presented in this study, I ask: has the Zetas' exposure on social media increased their

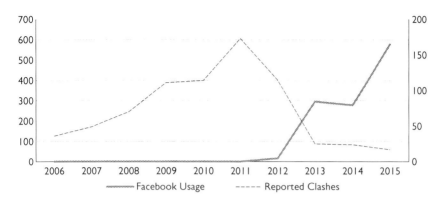

Graph 4.5 The Zetas' Facebook Usage and Reported Clashes 2006–2015.

vulnerability and therefore have they experienced more targeting by the security forces or rival groups? To approach this question, I evaluated the relationship between social media presence and reported clashes. Graph 4.5 shows the association between the two variables.

Overall, in the graph, the data does not exhibit a positive relationship between the use of social media and the behavioral pattern of the cartel's clashes. Table 4.1 displays the statistical correlation between the two variables.

The relationship between the two variables demonstrates a significant (at the 0.01 level) but negative correlation. A negative correlation tells us that as one variable goes up, the other one tends to go down or vice versa. In other words, as the use of social media increases, reported clashes in which the Zetas were involved diminish. However, since Pearson correlation coefficient values range from +1 to –1, a –0.386 is considered a weak correlation.

Table 4.1 Correlation between the Zetas' Facebook Presence and Reported Clashes

Correlations

		Facebook Use	Clashes
Facebook Use	Pearson Correlation	1	–0.386**
	Sig. (2-tailed)		0.000
	N	120	120
Clashes	Pearson Correlation	–0.386**	1
	Sig. (2-tailed)	0.000	
	N	120	120

Note
**Correlation is significant at the 0.01 (2-tailed).

Table 4.2 The Zetas Regression, Facebook Use

Model Summary

Model	R	R Square	Adjusted R Square	Std. Error of the Estimate	Change Statistics				
					R Square Change	F Change	df1	df2	Sig. F Change
1	0.386a	0.149	0.142	4.645	0.149	20.625	1	118	0.000

Note
a Predictors: (Constant), Facebook Use.

In Table 4.2, a regression between the two variables shows an $R^2 = 0.149$, indicating a close to 15 percent chance that the use of social media by the Zetas does not correspond to an increase of clashes. A 15 percent of explanation power is, once again, not that strong.

Since this case study has displayed different interplays between rivals and actors involved in the conflict, as the citizenship has been also reporting on the cartels, I wanted to consider if citizens' social media usage to expose the Zetas has had any impact on their clashes. For this, the use of a popular hashtag used by citizens in the state of Tamaulipas #*ValorporTamaulias* from 2012 and 2015 was monitored in Google trends, and the clashes reported in the state of Tamaulipas during the same period of time were considered. I chose this timeframe because April 2012 marks the first indication of the use of the hashtag. *Valor por Tamaulipas* is one of the portals created to report on the drug war happenings and on the cartels. Although active members and creators of webpages to report on the drug war have been assassinated, the Zetas' terrible menaces against cyber reporting have not been that effective, as people are still reporting on them, and 3,425 tweets were used to analyze this. Table 4.3 shows the results.

The outcome specifies that the use of the hashtag by civilians to report on the Zetas and the amount and frequency of clashes are not significantly correlated. The $R^2 = 0.013$ indicates that there is a 1.3 percent chance that the civilians reporting the Zetas on social media causes any type of impact on confrontations for the criminal organization. At least with this specific

Table 4.3 The Zetas Regression, Twitter Use

Model Summary

Model	R	R Square	Adjusted R Square	Std. Error of the Estimate
1	0.112a	0.013	−0.005	0.857

Note
a Predictors: (constant), Twitter.

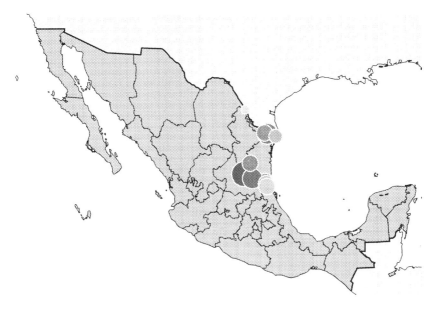

Map 4.1 Twitter Hashtag Usage per Region.
Source: Google Trends.

hashtag there is no indication of influence. Map 4.1 illustrates the regions in which the hashtag is mainly used. These municipalities include: Tula, Rio Bravo, Mante, Ciudad Victoria, Altamira, Miramar, Reynosa, Tampico, Matamoros, and Nuevo Laredo. All of these cities have been living under the Zetas' terror for almost a decade.

Conclusions

The Zetas broke with the traditional *modus operandi* of the Mexican cartels, diversifying their activities and adopting a more aggressive expansionist strategy, but they also have faced important internal problems, and probably made more enemies than any other criminal group in Mexico. At its beginning, the former armed wing of the Gulf cartel functioned under a military-hierarchical structure, and later restructured itself into a franchise framework. The new structural prototype was more decentralized and facilitated the creation of a more cellular configuration.

Particularly during the mandate of Felipe Calderón (2006–2012), the Zetas presented an extraordinary and unusual rate of growth. Also, during Calderón's administrations, the Zetas experienced more attacks by the government security forces than did other cartels. Paradoxically, this was the organization that grew the most within Mexico and expanded to other countries between 2010 and 2012 (Ravelo, 2013). The cartel's violent ways have gained them many more enemies to fight, including civilians, in comparison to other cases. After the death of Heriberto Lazcano, the cartel has weakened but it is still one of the most influential in the country, with a strong and deep intrinsic operational network that has not been weakened.

Like the Sinaloa cartel, the Zetas have implemented the use of social media in their strategies. But there are dissimilarities in the way the drug war and its dynamics have morphed throughout the war years in the areas where the Zetas operate. It is suggested here that social media became an instrument through which civilians became active participants in the drug war, directly attacking the Zetas by reporting on them in social media. This situation gradually progressed into a war of all against all: the Zetas killing civilians for reporting on Twitter or blogs, government incarcerating civilians for reporting, not forgetting the violations of human rights by the military, civilians organizing demonstrations claiming justice and security from the government, and civilians allying with Zetas' rivals to get rid of them.

The Zetas' usage and platform of choice is somewhat different from the Sinaloa cartel. This cartel has made more use of Facebook. Analogous to the Sinaloa cartel's Twitter network, the Zetas' Facebook network corresponds to the physical configuration they adopted later, presenting a highly decentralized structure. In addition, the data suggests that both cartels have used social media for public relations purposes. In the Sinaloa cartel, their social media environment and public response exhibited support from the citizenship; they are really admired and loved. People seek for their protection – even people living in other states such as Tamaulipas have asked for their help, as was earlier revealed in this chapter. The Zetas have made use of this strategy as well, but they have used it with the opposite purpose. One of the specificities in the way the cartel operates, and what has differentiated them from others, is how they function by fomenting terror. The Zetas love to be feared. Social media has been another outlet for them to spread their horror. Through the content on these platforms it can also be seen that they are successful at attracting young people to enlist in their workforce. They do this by demonstrating that by being part of the organization you will have a good paid job and will have some type of power "status." The *narcoraps* can work also as a tool of attraction, especially with young adults or teenagers being their biggest niche for recruitment from both sides of the border.

The results of the analysis in this chapter suggest that there is no strong evidence that the use of social media has made the Zetas cartel more exposed and an easier target for attacks. On the contrary, social media has successfully worked for the organization, establishing a powerful psychological warfare, instigating fear in society so they can conduct their business without intrusions. However, this case study shows that the Zetas present an important vulnerability, which was made obvious when the group Anonymous threatened them with exposure of their physical operations network through social media. The cartel quickly responded and succumbed to the activists' request, indicating that if used effectively, social media can also work as their Achilles heel.

Notes

1. As stated in a previous chapter, the term "traditional cartels" in this study refers to the *modus operandi* of the criminal organizations. Traditional cartels still followed the tacit agreements, for example, keeping violence away from innocent people. Non-traditional cartels like the Zetas do not follow such agreements and follow a more diverse illicit business portfolio.
2. The GAFES were created during the administration of Ernesto Zedillo Ponce de León (1994–2000), when the national security policy was focused towards reinforcing the security forces with elements of the Mexican military (Ravelo, 2013: p. 36).
3. Also known as the Continuing Criminal Enterprise or CCE Statute, a U.S. federal law that targets large-scale drug traffickers responsible for long-term and elaborate drug conspiracies. The sentence for a CCE conviction ranges from a minimum of 20 years in prison to a maximum of a life sentence. More legal details available at: www.law.cornell.edu/uscode/text/21/848.
4. These structural terms *military-hierarchical* and *franchise* are taken from a conversation with Dr. Bruce Bagley on March 17, 2017.
5. Video originally retrieved from: www.youtube.com/watch?v=uz6ko0R_yqU (unavailable by time of publication).
6. *Halcones*, or hawks, are people working for the organization who serve as informants or vigilantes on the streets.
7. Video available at: www.youtube.com/watch?v=knkjQpe9SVA.
8. Veronica Martin is a Colombian girl who posted a series of offensive tweets to the Mexican people during the passing of hurricane "Patricia." Her posts were retweeted by one of El Chapo's accounts in October 2015, and members of the Zetas sent their menacing messages as well. Chapo's tweet was originally retrieved from: https://twitter.com/elchap0guzman_/status/657784180328132609?lang=en (unavailable by the time of publication because of the suspension of El Chapo's account).
9. *Spanglish* refers to a hybrid language combining words and idioms from both Spanish and English (available at: www.lexico.com/definition/spanglish).
10. Syncretism refers to the amalgamation or attempted amalgamation of different religions, cultures, or schools of thought.
11. Sensitive image originally retrieved from: www.lanacion.com.ar/1406114-mexico-asesinados-y-colgados-por-denunciar-en-twitter-asuntos-narcos. The image may also be retrievable from: www.chicagotribune.com/hoy/ct-hoy-8031400-cuelgan-a-dos-e28098ciberperiodistase28099-por-denunciar-el-crimen-en-las-redes-sociales-story.html.
12. The tweets were translated by the author.

References

Beittel, J. S. (2013). *Mexico's drug trafficking organizations: Source and scope of the violence*. Congressional Research Service.

Castillo, E. (2015, March 4). Mexican police grab latest Zetas leader in wealthy suburbs. *The San Diego Union-Tribune*. Retrieved from: www.sandiedouniontribune.com/sdut-official-mexico-arrests-zetas-leader-omar-trevino-2015mar04-story.html.

CNN Mexico (2011). Auto de formal prision por terrorismo a 2 usuarios de Twitter en Veracruz. *Expansión*. August 31. Retrieved from: http://expansion.mx./nacional/2011/08/31/auto-de-formal-prision-por-terrorismo-a-2-usuarios-de-twitter-en-veracruz.

Congressional Research Service. (2019). *Mexico: Organized crime and drug trafficking organizations*. CRS Report. Retrieved from: https://fas.org/sgp/crs/row/R41576.pdf.

Correa-Cabrera, G. (2017). *Los Zetas Inc.: Criminal corporations, energy, and civil war in Mexico*. University of Texas Press.

Coscia, M., & Rios, V. (2012). *Knowing where and how criminal organizations operate using web content*. Maui, HI: CIKM'12.

Dudley, S., & Rios, V. (2013, September 1). La Marca Zeta. *Nexos*. Retrieved from: www.nexos.com.mx/?p=15461.

Frontline (2014). Family Tree. The Gulf Cartel. PBS. Retrieved from: www.pbs.org/wgbh/pages/frontline/shows/mexico/family/gulfcartel.html.

González, V. (2016, June 17). Autodefensas impiden secuestros en Tamaulipas. *Milenio*. Retrieved from:www.milenio.com/region/Autodefensas_impiden_secuestros_en_Tamaulipas-Villagran-Hudalgo_y_Mainero_0_757724512.html.

Grayson, G. W. (2014). *The cartels. The story of Mexico's most dangerous criminal organizations and their impact on U.S. security*. Santa Barbara, CA: Praeger.

Grayson, G. W., & Logan, S. (2017). *The executioner's men: Los Zetas, rogue soldiers, criminal entrepreneurs, and the shadow state they created*. Routledge.

Guzmán, J. M. (2016, November 25). Suman mas de 70 mil migrantes desaparecidos en Mexico: activistas. *El Universal*. Retrieved from: www.eluniversal.com.mx/articulo/estados/2016/11/25/suman-mas-de-70-mil-migrantes-desaparecidos-en-mexico-activistas.

Hernandez Herrera, O. (2014, March 2). La Huasteca vio nacer al fundador de "zetas." *Excélsior*. Retrieved from: www.hrw.org/world-report/2016/country-chapters/mexico#043288.

Human Rights Watch. (2016). *Mexico events of 2015*. World Report. Retrieved from: www.hrw.org/world-report/2016/country-chapters/mexico.

InSight Crime (2016a). Alejandro "Omar" Treviño Morales, alias "Z42." Retrieved from: www.insightcrime.org/mexico-organized-crime-news/omar-trevino-morales-alias-z-42/.

InSight Crime (2016b). Zetas. Retrieved on February 20, 2016 from: www.insightcrime.org/mexico-organized-crime-news/zetas-profile/.

La Verdad. (2019). Por qué el cártel de Sinaloa ha decidido apoyar a El Marro en su lucha contra el CJNG? November 11. Retrieved from: https://laverdadnoticias.com/crimen/Por-que-el-Cartel-de-Sinaloa-ha-decidido-apoyar-a-El-Marro-en-su-LUCHA-contra-el-CJNG-20191111-0038.html.

Pachico, E. (2012). "El Taliban" capture will not heal Zetas divide. InSight Crime. Retrieved from: www.insightcrime.org/news/analysis/el-taliban-capture-zetas-split/.

Paullier, J. (2016). Mexico: Asi ocurrio la brutal y olvidaa masacre de Allende, una de las mas sangrientas de Los Zetas. BBC News. Retrieved from: www.bbc.com/mundo/noticias-america-latina-37614215.

Pérez Salazar, J. C. (2015). Mexico: Como fue la captura de Omar Treviño, el brutal líder de los Zetas. *BBC Mundo*. March 5. Retrieved from: https://www.bbc.com/mundo/noticias/2015/03/150305_mexico_omar_trevino_z42_vida_caida_jcps.

Proceso (2016, March 16). Fraccion de los Zetas, ahora Cartel del Noreste, advierte massacre por extradiciones. *Proceso*. Retrieved from: www.proceso.com.mx/433674/fraccion-los-zetas-cambia-a-cartel-del-noreste-advierte-masacre-extraditan-al-z-40-z-42.

Ravelo, R. (2013). *Zetas: La franquicia criminal*. Mexico: EdicionesB.

Rios, V. (2012). *How government structure encourages criminal violence: The causes of Mexico's drug war*. Cambridge, MA: Harvard University.

Secretaria de Marina. (2011, December 13). Comunicado de Prensa 391/2011. Retrieved from: http://2006-2012.semar.gob.mx/sala-prensa/comunicados-2011/2016-comunicado-391-2011.html.

Soberanes, R. (2011). Auto de formal prisión por terrorismo a 2 usuarios de Twitter en Veracruz. *Expansión*. Retrieved from: https://expansion.mx/nacional/2011/08/31/auto-de-formal-prision-por-terrorismo-a-2-usuarios-de-twitter-en-veracruz.

Thorpe, H. (2013). Anatomy of a Drug Cartel. *Texas Monthly*, January 21. Retrieved from: www.texasmonthly.com/articles/anatomy-of-a-drug-cartel/.

Vega, A. (2011, September 19). Se alian cartels para pelear contra los Zetas. *Excélsior*. Retrieved from: www.excelsior.com.mx/2011/09/19/nacional/769062.

Chapter 5

The Caballeros Templarios

The Caballeros Templarios (CT) made their first appearance on March 8, 2011, after splitting from La Familia Michoacana (FM) cartel. Their arrival was announced on banners distributed throughout Michoacán, the Mexican state in which the criminal organization is mainly based, announcing the Templarios were going to take over the "altruist activities previously performed by La Familia," asserting that their mission was to protect the "sacred, free, and sovereign state of Michoacán" (InSight Crime, 2017a; Bunker & Sullivan, 2019).

La Familia Michoacana aligned with the Zetas when the group, still operating under the Gulf cartel, had the mission of training the organization to be their allies to control the *plaza* in Michoacán (Congressional Research Service, 2019). In 2006, La Familia decided to part from the Zetas and expelled them from Michoacán. They were against their abuses against the population and the violence reigning in the state. The new cartel stated that their mission was to protect the state from other criminal organizations that wanted to profit from the state's resources, including the Zetas (Congressional Research Service, 2019). By 2010, La Familia had established itself as one of the most powerful and bloodiest criminal organizations in Mexico. They infamously announced their arrival by throwing five human heads, presumably from Zetas members, onto the dance floor of a nightclub in Uruapan, Michoacán, on September 7, 2006 (Marquez, 2006). The cartel grew strong, building a wide methamphetamine distribution network, and conducted business in the Netherlands, India, China, and Bulgaria, and in various cities in the U.S. La Familia experienced a massive internal rupture after the supposed death of Nazario Moreno, their main leader and founder, and the organization's power and influence decreased significantly (InSight Crime, 2017a). After this, the Caballeros Templarios emerged.

The Caballeros Templarios cartel took their name from the medieval Knights Templar that fought during the crusades defending the Catholic faith in the twelfth and fourteenth centuries. This cartel differentiated themselves from the others in Mexico by their semi-religious ideology and rhetoric. There is some mysticism surrounding the cartel and their discourse was one of defendants and protectors of their land and people (Najar, 2014; Lomnitz, 2019; Kail, 2019; Bunker & Keshavarz, 2019).

By about 2013, the Caballeros Templarios were considered the third most powerful drug trafficking group in Mexico, just after the Sinaloa and the Zetas cartels. Besides their dominance in the state of Michoacán, they also have a presence in Edomex, Jalisco, and Morelia, states highly disputed by other criminal organizations (InSight Crime, 2017a). The Templarios grew at an accelerating rate, and in just two years the organization gained control of important territories in Michoacán. The cartel grew to be considered one of the most violent organizations in the country having inherited the *modus operandi* of La Familia (Najar, 2014; Congressional Research Service, 2019). After the capture of their last influential leader, Servando Gómez "La Tuta," in February 2015, the organization became considerably debilitated.

The Templarios adopted social media into their communication strategies. Indeed, the most famous Mexican *cybersicario*, "El Broly Banderas," was a member of this cartel (Cox, 2013). El Broly was a pioneer of the *sicarios*' practice of making their criminal lives public and attractive. Journals from all over the world have published entire articles devoted to the *sicario*. The usage of social media by the Templarios, however, differentiates them from other criminal groups.

This chapter centers on the Caballeros Templarios cartel. The first section presents the cartel's background, structure, and current status. The second evaluates the cartel's survival capacity by observing the way the Templarios respond to major organizational setbacks. The third section evaluates the organization's presence on and use of social media and examines the effect social media usage has on the cartel's confrontations. In the last part, I present the concluding remarks.

The Caballeros Templarios: A Narco-Sect

The state of Michoacán is a territory that has been, and still is, disputed by other strong drug trafficking organizations. Its location and geographical conditions make it attractive for cartels (InSight Crime, 2017a). In the south, the state borders the Pacific Ocean, holding one of the most important commercial ports in the Americas, the port of Lázaro Cárdenas which has served as a point of entry for cocaine from South America and chemical precursors from Asia for the production of methamphetamines, cocaine, and heroin (InSight Crime, 2017a). The port is a hub for commercial shipments that are distributed to the U.S., Canada, and Europe (Congressional Research Service, 2019). Michoacán also enjoys different climates and miles of mountainous territories ideal for the growing of limes, avocados, mango, and banana. Yet, the climatic conditions are also ideal for the plantation of marijuana and poppy crops. The region is also called *Tierra Caliente*

(Hot Land), in reference to the highly violent environment in the area, and is constantly battled over various groups (Infobae, 2019).

The state of Michoacán is known as well for political alternation, having different parties governing its 113 municipalities (Astorga, 2010). This has made the state–narco relationship complicated and violent. Michoacán is considered a weak state, or even a failed state, in regards to its institutional dysfunctionality and deep-rooted corruption (Castellanos, 2016), adding one more condition to the idyllic environment for organized crime to flourish and operate.

Before La Familia Michoacana, the group that used to control the drug business in the area was a group known as *El Milenio* (The Millennium) that worked alongside the Tijuana cartel (InSight Crime, 2017a). This relationship started to crumble when members of El Milenio felt abused by the outsider cartel exploiting their resources. Members of this group contacted the Gulf cartel to establish an alliance to take the Tijuana cartel out of Michoacán. The Gulf cartel sent their then armed wing, the Zetas. By 2003, the Zetas stood as the main cartel in the region. Members of El Milenio got training from them, but the locals did not support the vicious ways of the Zetas business model. During the following years, the Zetas put the Michoacanian communities through a lot of distress; resentment started building up once they expanded their methamphetamines production in the state. This is when La Familia appeared, founded by Nazario Moreno González, alias "El Chayo," in 2006 (Congressional Research Service, 2019).

There are various versions of what happened to this cartel. After the first alleged death of their messianic leader Nazario Moreno on December 9, 2010, the organization lost significant power. Some experts consider that La Familia mutated into the Templarios, only "changing their name" (Otero, 2011). There is another version, which states that La Familia continued operating under the leadership of José de Jesús Méndez "El Chango," one of its co-founders, but then disbanded completely after his capture in June 2011 (Morales & Rivera Ramirez, 2011).

As mentioned earlier, after the death of Nazario Moreno, La Familia experienced an internal rupture. In March, 2011, co-founders Enrique Plancarte Solís "El Kike," Servando Gómez "La Tuta," and Diosinio Loya Plancarte "El Tio," formed a new group, the Caballeros Templarios. A great part of the members of La Familia left to be part of the new cartel (InSight Crime, 2017a).

In the beginning, following La Familia's religious path, the Caballeros Templarios were founded as a kind of a cartel-sect. Their recruitment tactics were strict. To get accepted as part of the Templarios, an application including a picture had to be reviewed by the Council, formed by the founders. If accepted, the members had to pledge to the organization for life. The new recruits were initiated in rituals (Najar, 2014; Lomnitz, 2019).

The Caballeros Templarios cartel aimed to construct an image of honor and altruism around their organization; their main mission was to "fight and die for social justice" (Keene, 2019: p. 66). They followed an ethical code, "The Code of the Caballeros Templarios of Michoacán" (Kail, 2019; Najar, 2014). When entering the organization, the new recruits were given a 22-page booklet containing the rules they must follow, the group's ideology, and procedures. In their inauguration ceremonies, the new members pledged to help the poor, fight against materialism, respect women and children, not to kill for money, and were prohibited from using drugs. The cartel went as far as conducting random drug testing (BBC Mundo, 2012). If rules were broken, offenders would pay with their own lives. The Templarios also opened clinics to treat addictions; these centers later served as a major source for recruitment. The organization granted loans to farmers, and they also built schools and churches throughout the region in an attempt to gain the support of the community (Congressional Research Service, 2019).

Structure and Modus Operandi

The Templarios inherited a pyramidal semi-religious structure from La Familia (Reyez, 2014). Every leader had a specific rank in the organization. At the top they had four leaders,[1] Nazario Moreno, Enrique Plancarte Solís, Servando Gómez, and Diosinio Loya Plancarte; next on the ladder were 100 *plaza* leaders, and at the base about 500 *sicarios* (Reyez, 2014).

Their *modus operandi* shifted with time. Illegal activities that were previously prohibited under their code of ethics, such as extortion and kidnappings, became a great source of income for the cartel. Another big part of their profits came from coercion like *cobro de piso* or *cobro por protección*.[2] Eighty-five percent of formal businesses in Michoacán were obliged to pay for this "service" (InSight Crime, 2017a) as the Templarios came to dominate the economy and production in their main areas of influence. This practice caused the closing of many local businesses and the flight of hundreds of Michoacanians to other states. Alternative profits came from paid executions, including political assassinations (Reyez, 2014).

The cartel uses propaganda techniques to generate a climate of social intimidation to amplify the margin of impunity under which they operate and justify their criminal conduct. At the same time, they somehow try to maintain their image of benefactors and vigilantes, often proclaimed by their leaders. To achieve their objectives, they resort to highly violent tactics that have victimized entire communities. Violence towards authorities and citizens has been a fundamental part of their operative logic (Otero, 2011).

The Caballeros Templarios Today

After the capture of the last standing leader Servando Gómez "La Tuta," the organization weakened significantly and lost its influence, but remnants of the organization still exist across the state of Michoacán (Bunker & Keshavarz, 2019). The vulnerability of the powerful cartel has opened a vacuum for other criminal organizations to take over the *plaza en Michoacán*. According to a report from the Congressional Research Service (2019), there are new spinoff groups or fragments of other cartels filling the void the Templarios have left, including the rise of groups as *Los Viagras* (LV) and Cartel Jalisco Nueva Generación that are fighting to take over the municipalities close to the port of Lázaro Cárdenas. In March 2017, the leader of Los Viagras, José Carlos Sierra Santana, was killed. This has created a "bloodbath as cartels struggled to assert new patterns of dominance" (p. 25). In addition to the CJNG and Los Viagras, there are several other criminal cells battling with alarming violence for the control of the state, such as: *La Nueva Familia Michoacana*, *El Grupo del Cenizo*, and *El Brazo de Oro* (Infobae, 2019).

Survival Capacity

Michoacán, native state of former president Felipe Calderón, was the region that received the first wave of troops deployed, a total of 6,500 elements, soon after he announced the militarization of the war on drugs in 2006. Also known as *Operacion Michoacán*, this action marked the starting point of the conflict (Grillo, 2006).

Three years later, in July 2009, the Secretary of National Defense (SEDENA) sent an additional 2,500 military elements to reinforce the security forces in the state. In 2013, Peña Nieto sent 5,000 more elements from the military and the police were deployed to the state to fortify, once again, the fight against the drug cartels (Pineda, 2013).

In this context, Michoacán is one of the states that throughout the drug war years has presented a higher degree of militarization and violence. It has not only faced strong military presence, and violent drug cartels fighting for turf, but also, the state has witnessed the creation of paramilitary self-defense groups. Citizens from farmers to businessmen and from different towns experiencing abuses and terror from the Templarios created the groups. They did not feel the federal or local police were protecting them. One main leader of the self-defense movement was José Manuel Mireles Valverde "El Doctor" (The Doctor). On February 24, 2013, the first group was established in the municipalities of Tepalcatepec and Buenavista Tomatlan, in *Tierra Caliente*. For some time, the government supported these groups, as they grew stronger and gained influence. They were able to deliver heavy blows to the criminal organization and accomplished what the government could not: that is, banishing the Caballeros Templarios from their towns, and regaining control and peace, at least for a while (Congressional Research Service, 2019).

Nonetheless, despite the high concentration of security forces and self-defense groups, the state has been the cradle of two of the most powerful organizations in the country, namely, La Familia and the Caballeros Templarios. Subsequently, these two criminal groups have not enjoyed the same fate as their rivals, the Sinaloa and the Zetas cartels, as they have become considerably debilitated. How did the Caballeros Templarios manage to get to the top of the drug trafficking industry so rapidly, with the high concentration of security forces, the pressure of rival cartels, and the constant attacks of self-defense militia groups in Michoacán? What led to their accelerated debilitation?

In this section, the survival capacity of the Caballeros Templarios is studied. Assessing which actors target them the most and the regularity of their attacks gives a good indication of the landscape in which the cartel operated and the symmetry or asymmetry of their enemies in terms of capabilities. In addition, I present an analysis of the Templarios' response to major organizational setbacks.

Confrontations

As earlier stated, the war on drugs in the state of Michoacán developed into an extremely violent conflict. There was a high concentration of military forces fighting the violent drug cartels, and cartels battling each other. In addition, the expansion of self-defense militia groups and their growing influence throughout the state during 2013 and 2015, added another level to the violence since all of these actors were highly armed.

Graph 5.1 shows the confrontations the cartel faced from its beginnings in 2011 to 2015. I gathered the data from *El Universal*'s archives. This study is based on 96 reports of incidents in which the Templarios were specifically involved. The graph illustrates the different actors fighting the Templarios and their share of confrontations.

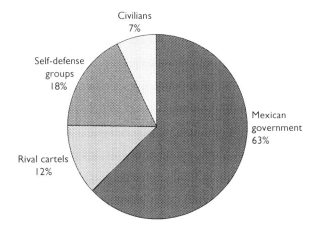

Graph 5.1 Caballeros Templarios' Reported Clashes 2011–2015.

The data shows that government security forces have been responsible for 63 percent of the clashes the Caballeros Templarios have been involved in since the organization began to operate. The federal police is the security body that has mostly targeted the organization, followed by the military. The next actors on their list of enemies are the self-defense groups. In the cases of the Sinaloa cartel and the Zetas, rival cartels were usually the second biggest adversaries for the criminal organization. Nevertheless, in the case of the Templarios, the self-defense groups became their second biggest enemy. But these once-united forces, fighting for a common interest, started to antagonize each other, causing fragmentation. Some of the self-defense groups joined cartels other than the Templarios or started cooperating with outside criminal organizations, such as Cartel Jalisco Nueva Generación. In March 2014, the government captured self-defense leader of La Ruana, Hipólito Mora, who was accused of participating in the homicides of two members of other self-defense groups (*Guardian*, 2014). Later, on June 27, 2014, the Mexican authorities arrested Mireles Valverde, founder of one militia group. With this, some self-defense groups dissolved and members went back to their normal lives, only to find themselves and their families menaced by retaliation from the Caballeros Templarios. There is a debate over whether the militias or vigilante groups in Michoacán can be considered heroes, for "freeing communities" from criminal organizations, or villains, since some of the groups have gone over to illicit business (Grillo, 2014).

The third actors the Templarios confronted the most were rival cartels, with 12 percent of the share. The Zetas and the Cartel Jalisco Nueva Generación stand as the criminal organizations with which the Templarios had major tensions. Lastly, 7 percent is made up of clashes with civilians. In the previous chapter, the Zetas' case presented a similar trend of civilians emerging as an active player and as a target in the drug war. This tendency shows again in this case, but not with the Sinaloa cartel. It is important to highlight that younger criminal organizations tend to follow a non-traditional *modus operandi*. The case of the Caballeros Templarios is multifaceted. The organization, in its beginnings, established a strict code of ethics, violation of which was penalized with death. What is more, its members pledged to protect civilians; it was against the rules to kill innocent people. My data shows, nevertheless, that this principle started to be broken just a year after the group first appeared. This implies a change in the cartel's *modus operandi* from a traditional, semi-religious cult to a non-traditional group like the Zetas.

Caballeros Templarios Response to Organizational Shocks

After La Familia lost its power and the Caballeros Templarios started rising, the cartel became the priority target of federal and state security forces (Otero, 2011). Then the group also became the main target of the self-defense groups around 2013 and 2014. In contrast to the cases presented up to now in this book, the Templarios were not as effective in coping with the constant attacks. This subsection studies the main organizational setbacks the organization has suffered. I monitored their criminal activities throughout the attacks in order to observe their behavioral response to major organizational shocks.

The Caballeros Templarios emerged in 2011, but it was not until 2014 that the cartel started receiving their most important setbacks. The first important disruption for the Templarios was the capture of Dionisio Loya Plancarte "El Tio." He was arrested by elements of the Mexican army and the PGR in the state of Michoacán on January 27, 2014. El Tio played a key role in La Familia, and then in the Templarios. Garay Salamanca and Salcedo-Albarán (2011), conducted a social network analysis to recreate the physical network of La Familia cartel. El Tio registered as the most central node concentrating the largest quantity of direct social relationships. He served as the public relations person in La Familia, and later in the Templarios. Loya Plancarte was in charge of articulating and establishing agreements with public servants at various levels. El Tio was considered the third in command in the structure of the Templarios (InSight Crime, 2017a). Two months later, the organization received its greatest setback yet. Nazario Moreno, also known as "El Chayo," or "El Mas Loco" (the Craziest One), the top messianic leader of the organization, lost his life (for the second time) during a confrontation with the Mexican marines and army elements in Tumbiscatío, Michoacán, on March 9, 2014. Nazario Moreno started in the drug trafficking business working for the Milenio cartel and he operated in the Mexican-American border area of Tamaulipas and Texas. After being arrested by the U.S. authorities in McAllen, Texas a couple of times, he moved to the state of Michoacán and established La Familia with co-founder José de Jesús Méndez Vargas "El Chango." Nazario Moreno is considered a pseudo-religious leader who presumably indoctrinated members of his criminal organization through gospels. By 2009, the federal government, then under Calderón's mandate, offered a $2.4 million reward in exchange for information that led to his capture. The following year, in 2010, the government announced his alleged death during a shootout with the federal security forces, but his body was not recovered. It was four years later that his passing was officially confirmed. This time, the authorities were in possession of his lifeless body and matching DNA. He died a day after his forty-fourth birthday (*Excélsior*, 2014).

A third significant organizational setback came with the assassination of Enrique Plancarte Solís, also known as "El Kike." He was killed in a joint operation by the marines and the army on March 31, 2014, in the municipality of Colón, in the state of Querétaro. El Kike was also one of the founders of La Familia who then held a higher rank within the Templarios. He was the financial leader in charge of coordinating the production of methamphetamines for the organization (Najar, 2014). Numerous homicides have been attributed to this leader, some of them victims of the religious rituals, a usual practice of the organization.

After these three main organizational disruptions, just one original leader remained, Servando Gómez "La Tuta." A manhunt for the last standing capo by the Mexican authorities lasted a couple of years. Finally, he was captured by an elite police force on February 27, 2015. La Tuta was originally a schoolteacher in the community of Arteaga, Michoacán, before he decided to join the drug trafficking world. As the public face of the organization, he fervently promoted the organization's ideology of vigilantes for their communities. He often claimed that the Caballeros Templarios' ultimate mission was to protect Michoacán from groups like the Zetas and had grievances with the federal police for their countless violations of human rights. La Tuta or "El Profe" (the Professor) was also in charge of coordinating drug shipments through Baja California (InSight Crime, 2017b). His arrest was considered one of the biggest victories of the government against this organization, bringing with it the end of the Caballeros Templarios as a powerful cartel. Figure 5.1 illustrates the major organizational setbacks discussed above, and the organization's response to them.

Theory and historical indicators suggest that hierarchical or pyramidal criminal organizations are more susceptible to strategies like the kingpin.

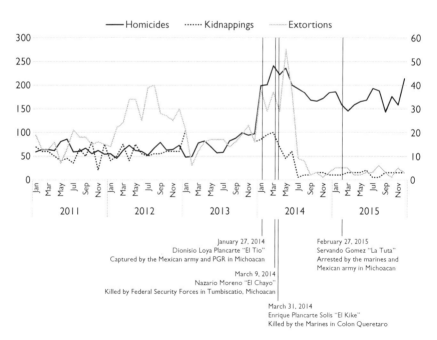

Figure 5.1 Caballeros Templarios' Response to Organizational Shocks 2011–2015.

Once the cupola of the cartel is taken down, violence erupts, the organization loses direction, experiences fragmentation and internal fracturing, and, lastly, it dissolves into less powerful criminal cells. Based on the model presented above, the Caballeros Templarios experienced such a fate.

The data shows that from 2011 to mid-2014, the Caballeros Templarios were functioning smoothly, indicators of violence and criminal activities remained steady, and extortions particularly high. Then, 2014 appears to have been a challenging year. During this time, the Templarios suffered three out of the four most critical setbacks, and that same year, the self-defense groups got stronger, really affecting the Templarios' strength. This can explain the rise of violence and criminal activities shown in the model above during this time of turmoil.

Despite the setbacks, the organization continued functioning under the leadership of the last standing leader, La Tuta. After his capture in February 2015, the Templarios presented signs of weakening. Their indicators of criminal activities, extortions and kidnappings, dropped significantly while violence erupted. A high rate of violence can be an indicator of intra-cartel confrontations and of rival groups taking advantage of the vulnerability of the cartel to take over turf. There are no signs of a restructuring within the organization; there are no hints of a strong leader taking over the organization. Their criminal activities remained low after the last shock, suggesting that they could not regain the strength they once held. The next section covers the presence on and usage of social media by the Templarios, assessing the influence this variable has had on their survival capacity.

Caballeros Templarios' Social Media Usage

As previously mentioned, the Caballeros Templarios got a lot of attention on social media during the cartel's early years, thanks to Antonio Olalde, better known as "El Broly Banderas" and considered "the most famous sicario on social media" (Cox, 2013). El Broly served as a personal guard to Servando Gómez "La Tuta." He started this practice of going public on Facebook while he was working as a *sicario* for La Familia cartel. Later, he followed his leaders and became a member of the Templarios. He was one of the pioneers of the Mexican *cybersicarios*' practice of uploading selfies, flaunting a lifestyle of extravagances, excesses and violence (Cox, 2013). El Broly posted selfies with kidnapped victims in the background, burned bodies, and pictures of piles of dead bodies left in the aftermath of a confrontation.[3] He was considered the bloodiest *sicario*. The case of El Broly has been reported in journals all over the world. There are about 25 profiles on Facebook under his name and identity. While examining all the open profiles, none of them seemed real. There is a possibility that his "official" account has been closed. Suddenly, El Broly dropped from the social media radar, and neither authorities nor self-defense groups really know what happened to him. Authorities believe he died during a shootout against the self-defense groups in 2015, and so his death was never made official (Lucio, 2015).

As members of the Templarios attracted public attention through Facebook, one of its main leaders, La Tuta, started using YouTube extensively as the outlet to spread his messages. This practice distinguishes the Templarios' social media strategies from those adopted by other cartel leaders. This section explores the Caballeros Templarios on Facebook and YouTube.[4] I present an examination of their social media presence, usage, content, and purpose of use. Finally, the relationship between the usage of social media on Facebook and YouTube and the organization's clashes is assessed.

Social Media Usage and Presence on Facebook

The Caballeros Templarios had a robust presence on Facebook at least until 2015, the last year this study covers. A social network analysis was conducted in order to visualize the cartel's online constitution, reach, and central nodes. Figure 5.2 is a simplified representation of the Templarios' Facebook network.

This network is composed of 188 edges and 57 vertices, totaling 24,990 friends and followers and it is divided into three main clusters or groups. When analyzing these groups, the configuration and origins of the cartel can

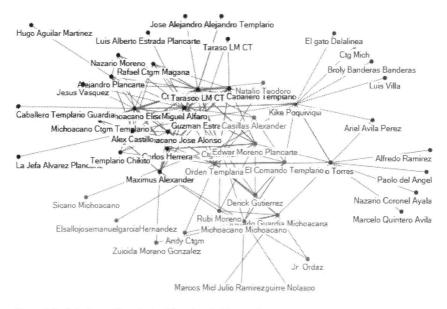

Figure 5.2 Caballeros Templarios' Facebook Network.

Source: Created with NodeXL Pro (http://nodexl.codeplex.com) from the Social Media Research Foundation (www.smrfoundation.org)

be traced, from their relation to the Zetas to their transition from La Familia to the Templarios. Group 3 (G3) is formed by members of rival cartels, though the majority of the profiles are from Zetas members, responsible for training La Familia Michoacana. In this case, the Facebook networks of the Zetas and the Templarios intertwined. For example, Ariel Avila, the most central node on the Zetas' Facebook network, studied in the previous chapter, is connected to this cluster. Group 2 (G2) highlights the transition process of members from La Familia to the Templarios. The profiles of this group show some element of affiliation to the emerging cartel, directly stating that they worked for La Familia before, but are currently working for the Caballeros Templarios. Group 1 (G1) is formed by just members of the Caballeros Templarios, demonstrating a full transition from one group to another. The node with the highest centrality in this network is that of Miguel Alfaro CT, followed by Tarasco LM CT, and *Orden Templaria*. Alfaro's and Tarasco's accounts are located in G1 and Orden Templaria in G2. The vertex with the higher degree of betweenness is Kike Poquiviqui. This node serves as a structural bridge holding the three clusters together and it seems that he has been one of the members that experienced the complete journey within the organization, from training with the Zetas to becoming part of the Caballeros Templarios.

This network does not mirror the pyramidal structure the cartel holds in the physical realm. A possible explanation for this is that the leaders at the top are not participants in this network. It does reflect the brotherhood ideology of the cartel. Cluster G1 is where the members of the Caballeros Templarios are concentrated the most; it is a closed group, and the links and communication among the members of this group show they have a close relationship. As in other cases, the members of cartels do communicate with each other over these platforms. In some of their posts, they tag each other in mission-related messages; other times, they talk in key or coded messages. The Caballeros Templarios' messages towards each other are focused on their bond as Templarios, and they treat each other like family, as brothers.

Content Analysis: Facebook

The content of the Facebook accounts of the Caballeros Templarios is similar to the content from the other cartels studied here. The profiles chosen for the analysis were based on their degree of centrality in the network and or being vertices with the highest betweenness. The most central nodes are the profiles that have the greatest concentration of edges, in other words the accounts of the Caballeros Templarios with a higher concentration of friends and followers. The nodes with a high degree of betweenness are vital nodes on a network because they are the ones that link the network together. I present the data gathered from these accounts in Graph 5.2.

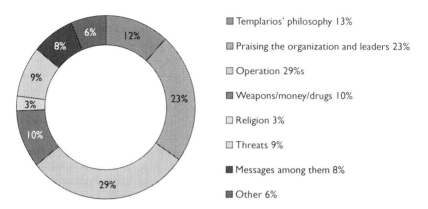

Graph 5.2 Caballeros Templarios' Facebook Content Analysis.

The content of the Facebook accounts of members of the Caballeros Templarios is divided into seven main categories. The main purpose of use for this group is posting about operations with 29 percent of the content. As in the other cases, these posts show pictures of members of the Templarios ready to complete a mission. Other posts are just statements, commenting on something about their assignment, a particular target, or a particular place.

The next category, with 23 percent, consists of posts related to praising the organization and their leaders. It does not come as a surprise that this category is a core part of the content due to the indoctrination imposed on their recruits. Praising the organization and honoring their leaders, especially Nazario Moreno and La Tuta, is a big part of their ritual traditions. The next type of post is related to the previous category, as 12 percent of the content in the Templarios accounts consists of posts about the philosophies of the cartel. Here, they quote biblical references and motivational sayings taken from the booklet they are given when they become an active member of the organization. Moreover, in these posts the Templarios talk about glory, honor, and humility, which is a great part of their ideological orientation and discourse – although their practices and actions contradict their rhetoric.

Next, with 10 percent, are posts and pictures of weapons, piles of money, and drugs. In these posts, the cartel members show their capabilities and their success in the drug trafficking industry, demonstrating strength and power to their rivals. Nine percent of the content consists of threats among the Caballeros Templarios, the Zetas, the Cartel Jalisco New Generation and the self-defense groups. The following category includes messages that they sent to each other, with 8 percent. As seen in the social network analysis, members of this cartel seem to develop strong ties that are reflected in these types of posts. "Other" categories, such as parties, pictures of dead bodies, and messages honoring members that lost their lives during battles,

Table 5.1 Correlation between Caballeros Templarios' YouTube Presence and Reported Clashes

Model Summary

Model	R	R Square	Adjusted R Square	Std. Error of the Estimate
1	0.147	0.022ª	−0.005	1.974

Note
a Predictors: (Constant), Facebook Use.

account for 6 percent of the content. Lastly, 3 percent are posts about religion. As noted before, religion is an important element of their identity. Most of the images here are pictures of altars dedicated to Nazario Moreno "El Chayo," who was canonized by the group and serves as the main saint they pray to, asking for protection.

Finally, the regression (Table 5.1) presents an R^2 of 0.02, meaning that there is a 2 percent chance that the usage of Facebook by cartel members is causing an increase in their clashes with authorities, rival cartels, or self-defense groups.

Content Analysis: YouTube

The Templarios' usage of YouTube sets them apart from the other cartels examined in this book. The criminal organization has a significant presence on YouTube considering that the organization is several years younger than the Sinaloa cartel or the Zetas. There are 51,400 videos related to the Caballeros Templarios available, with a significant proportion of the videos being documentaries related to the original medieval Knights Templar. The videos considered for the content analysis in this case total 531. Graph 5.3 shows the shares of content for this cartel on YouTube.

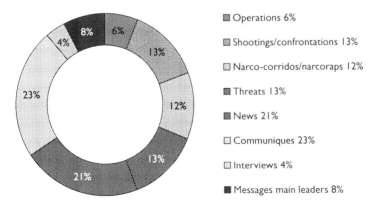

Graph 5.3 Caballeros Templarios' YouTube Content Analysis.

Most of the videos of the Caballeros Templarios on YouTube are communiques, accounting for 23 percent of the content. As in the other cases, these messages share a fair amount of information about the cartel. For example, structural changes to the organization are revealed. Also, associations between politicians and the Templarios are exposed. The cartel reports on future operations, warning civilians of the upcoming violence. These videos maintain a degree of anonymity since the communiques are generated through robotic voices. Most of these videos are provided by channels or blogs that have closely followed the war on drugs such as *Grillonautas* and *Blog del Narco*.

The second type of content is *narconews* with 21 percent. The news comes from traditional media stations. Excelsior TV is the source offering most of these reports. International newscasts such as Univision show clips related to the cartel. The items they present include news about organizational setbacks like the capture or killing of leaders, videos of La Tuta, battles or violent acts, or reports of arrested members.

The next two categories, each with 13 percent, are videos of live battles and shootings, and threats. The images from the battles and their aftermath are brutal. Some are from confrontations with rival cartels or self-defense groups, and others from those with government security forces. There is footage of a battle in which the Templarios managed to shoot down a Black Hawk used by the Mexican military to search and target criminal groups settled in the middle of the mountains. The share of threatening messages follows a similar pattern to the previous case studies, sending threatening messages to rival cartels or the government. In the case of the Caballeros Templarios, the interchanges take place mainly with the Cartel Jalisco Nueva Generación, the authorities, and self-defense groups. The groups involved in this exchange of threatening messages deliver long, planned speeches in which they explain their activities in an attempt to justify their actions. Demonstrations of tortures, beheadings, or executions are not a tactic that the Templarios resort to too often on this platform, so there are only a couple of videos displaying Zetas-style interrogations. *Narcocorridos* and *narcoraps* make up 12 percent of the content on YouTube.

The next category corresponds to messages sent directly by the organization leaders, with 8 percent of the content. These are mostly videos of La Tuta and there are two videos of El Tio, then the third in command of the cartel.[5] The footage of these videos follows a similar discourse and purpose, exposing authorities and reiterating that their organization works for the protection of the state of Michoacán and its inhabitants. The content of these videos is discussed in the next section in more depth. There is also just one very short video by El Broly, the popular *sicario*, sending greetings to his fans and followers.[6]

The last two types of content are operations, with 6 percent, and interviews with the final 4 percent. The interviews presented here are conversations with civilians either asking for help from the government or describing the violent conditions in which they have been forced to live, surrounded by cartels, military, and self-defense groups, all fighting for their own particular interests. In the interviews, it is obvious that the government has not been in anyway proactive in protecting civilians or in fighting criminal groups, especially in the *Tierra Caliente* region. These videos present testimonies of citizens living in exploited communities in which once high-flying businesses have been obliged to close, since they have been victims of commercial blockades. They state that there is a shortage of basic medicines, gasoline, and food because the Caballeros Templarios have prevented the flow of products into these communities. The consequences of such acts spread to other countries when there was a shortage of lemons and avocados in the U.S. and the rest of Mexico. Civilians state that the Templarios control the flow of trade goods in the area, charge fees, or business taxes, better known as *cobro de piso*, and have raised the price of basic products like tortillas in order to profit from them. This situation has ad a detrimental impact on the region's economy.

La Tuta on YouTube

It seems as if La Tuta enjoyed the attention he received with his YouTube videos reaching millions of viewers. He continued this practice throughout his leadership of the Templarios, with no intentions of maintaining any sort of anonymity. He made a total of 24 videos in a period of three years. His first appearance on YouTube was on August 24, 2012.[7] In the footage, he is sitting at a desk with a saint-like statue of Nazario Moreno, a black cross, similar to the ones used by the Knights Templar in the middle ages, a Mexican flag, and framed pictures of famous revolutionaries such as "El Che" Guevara and Pancho Villa. Also on his desk there is a pile of "Code of the Caballeros Templarios" booklets. In this video, he explains when the cartel was created and its purposes. He declares that the Caballeros Templarios are neither a drug cartel nor criminals. He proclaims that their mission is to protect people from the abuses of other criminal groups, the military, and the federal police, to protect their land, and to regulate violence. The same logic and tone to his discourse are evident on all his frequent appearances on YouTube.

In another video, uploaded in January 2014, La Tuta is walking around a kiosk in the municipal *plaza* of Tumbiscatío, Michoacán, giving cash away to the inhabitants of the community, inviting the population to join the Caballeros Templarios.[8] Portraying the organization as the Robin-Hood type, this is a strategy or *modus operandi* traditional drug cartels practice. The goal is to gain the support of the communities they operate in; this way, they can conduct their business without resistance, which is an important asset for criminal organizations. For the Caballeros Templarios, the strategy might have worked at first. With time, however, the cartel became just about everything they said they were standing against. They forgot all about codes, values, honor, and rules, and became violent and ruthless just like the Zetas, a group they regularly condemned for their gruesome business model.

There is another popular video of La Tuta uploaded on August 11, 2013, with more than three million views at the time of writing, in which he is giving an interview for an unidentified media outlet.[9] The interview takes place somewhere in the mountains in Michoacán, and the main purpose of the dialogue is for La Tuta to "clean" the bad image and reputation that, according to him, the media has created around his organization. During this interview, his discourse in relation to the doings of the Templarios starts to shift. The former professor states that his organization is "a necessary evil." Here he publicly accepts that his organization is criminal, but still benevolent and "needed." He continues arguing that they protect Michoacán from other "more vicious" groups such as the Zetas and the Cartel Jalisco New Generation. He also states that the Templarios defend the population from the military, the federal police's abuses, and other authorities that he refers to as delinquents; "this is a war of criminal against criminals," he states. Image 5.1 presents an image of the video just described.

Other videos serve different purposes. In one of them, La Tuta is publicly distributing the inheritance of a local landowner, getting a donation of 400,000 pesos (approximately $20,000 dollars) for the Caballeros Templarios.[10] The content of this video gives us an idea of the social and judicial roles La Tuta played in the communities under the Templarios' influence, serving as the de facto state. On some other videos, he publicly exposed politicians with ties with the drug cartel. The footage worked as evidence leading to the arrest and imprisonment of various political figures in Michoacán, such as Salma Karrum Cervantez, former mayor of Pátzcuaro, Michoacán,[11] and politician Vallejo Mora.[12]

Later, there was a shift in La Tuta's YouTube strategy. The last messages he sent through this platform were just audios. He explained that he wanted to get plastic surgery to change his face, just like *El Señor de los Cielos*, in order to avoid detection.[13] February 1, 2015 marks the official farewell of La Tuta from YouTube.[14] In his last official message, the former leader accuses authorities and rival cartels, confesses his illegal endeavors, asks for forgiveness for all the damage and suffering their organization has caused to the state of Michoacán, and sends his blessings. This audio has been reproduced 383,119 times. The fact that La Tuta started recording and uploading just audios instead of videos hints at the leader's state of mind and the pressure the organization was facing at the time, as if he felt trapped. He may have perceived that his over-the-top exposure on social media was having negative repercussions for their organization and increasing his detectability. Nevertheless, the change in tactic came too late. He was captured three weeks after his last uploaded message.

The Caballeros Templarios 121

Image 5.1 Nuevo comunicado de 'La Tuta' y Los Caballeros Templarios. Agosto 10, 2013.
Source: www.youtube.com/watch?v=adz_IDG0fKw.

La Tuta opted to use the platform in such a way that he was overly exposed. The technique might work in the sense that it is a more direct way to get a message across, appear more relatable, be "closer" to the people. Did La Tuta's social media tactic cause the organization to be more visible and therefore more targeted? This question is evaluated next.

YouTube Usage and Major Organizational Shocks

Figure 5.3 illustrates the activity on YouTube, conducted principally by La Tuta. As in the other cases, the use of social media increases significantly after the censorship of traditional media outlets. The utilization of the web-based platforms by Servando Gómez increases at specific instances, for example, during the capture or killing of three of the main leaders of the organization: Dionisio Loya Plancarte, Nazario Moreno, and Enrique Plancarte Solís. All of these setbacks occurred in a period of three months in 2014. In the figure, it can be observed that after these major organizational setbacks and before his capture, La Tuta was highly active on the social media platform. His last activity is registered just days before his capture.

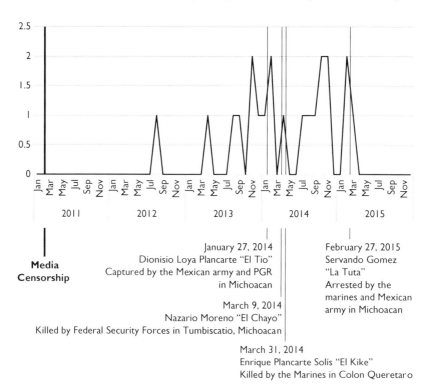

Figure 5.3 Caballeros Templarios' YouTube Usage and Major Organizational Shocks 2011–2015.

The Analysis

This section examines the relationship between the use of social media and the clashes the Templarios faced from 2011 to 2015. I conducted the study on two platforms, Facebook and YouTube. I then ran correlation statistical analyses in order to evaluate the relationship between the two variables.

Clashes and Facebook Usage

Graph 5.4 shows the relationship between the Facebook usage of the Caballeros Templarios members and reported clashes.

The correlation indicates that the two variables have a positive relationship but the association between them does not show any statistical significance, indicating a weak relationship. In other words, the usage of Facebook by the Templarios has not made the cartel more vulnerable or more exposed since reported clashes do not seem to increase because of their social media activity. As has been established throughout this chapter, the Templarios also have a presence on YouTube, with a similar extent to that of the Sinaloa and the Zetas cartels. Yet, the way they implemented it into their strategies sets them apart from the other two criminal organizations. Next, I study the relationship between the usage of YouTube and reported clashes.

Clashes and YouTube Usage

The nature of the YouTube platform is different from that of Twitter or Facebook, since the degree of anonymity can be compromised. YouTube is based on videos, footage that sometimes gives away more clues than

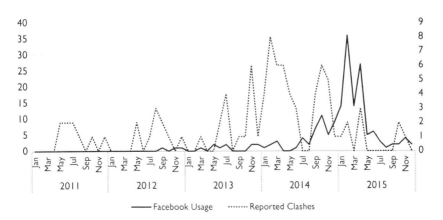

Graph 5.4 Caballeros Templarios' Reported Clashes and Facebook Use 2011–2015.

intended about the surroundings in which the video has been filmed, such as interiors, exteriors, light, or sounds. Nonetheless, it is completely possible to maintain secrecy if there is an intent to do so. For example, when shooting videos the group Anonymous International use masks, and edit their videos with voice regulators to maintain confidentiality. This was not a strategy leaders of the Templarios practiced. La Tuta uploaded a series of videos with no intention of protecting his identity. Did La Tuta's usage of YouTube benefit the Templarios, or, on the contrary, work against them? To answer this question, I analyzed the relationship between the cartel's exposure on YouTube and reported clashes. To achieve this, the series of videos of La Tuta on YouTube were considered for the analysis. Graph 5.5 illustrates the relationship between the variables.

The graph reveals a positive relationship between social media use and clashes. Table 5.2 exhibits the correlation values. The Pearson correlation coefficient indicates a positive 53 percent relationship between the variables with a (2-tailed) 0.01 significance level, meaning that the correlation indicates moderate statistical significance. In other words, increases in YouTube presence are significantly related to upsurges in clashes.

It is evident that in the case of the Templarios, the exposure of their main leader on YouTube had a negative impact on the survival capacity of the cartel. This finding suggests that the utilization of this particular social media platform by the Templarios increased their exposure, leading to greater targeting and therefore compromising their survival capacity. In addition, Table 5.3 presents the outcomes of a regression run between the two variables. The results show that there is a 28 percent chance that the increase in the amount of the clashes the Caballeros Templarios faced was caused by an increase of YouTube usage by La Tuta.

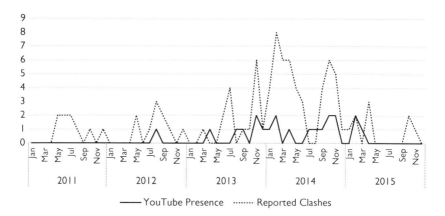

Graph 5.5 Caballeros Templarios' Reported Clashes and YouTube Usage 2011–2015.

Table 5.2 Caballeros Templarios Regression, Facebook Use

Correlations

		YouTube	Clashes
YouTube	Pearson Correlation	1	0.533**
	Sig. (2-tailed)		0.000
	N	60	60
Clashes	Pearson Correlation	−0.533**	1
	Sig. (2-tailed)	0.000	
	N	60	60

Note
**Correlation is significant at the 0.01 level (2-tailed).

Table 5.3. Caballeros Templarios Regression, YouTube Use

Model Summary

Model	R	R Square	Adjusted R Square	Std. Error of the Estimate
1	0.533[a]	0.284	−0.272	1.688

Note
a Predictors: (constant), YouTube.

Conclusions

The state of Michoacán combines geographical characteristics and climate conditions suitable for the proliferation of the drug trafficking business and the emergence of strong drug cartel organizations. Michoacán is also considered a failed or weak state. Whether this is an accurate statement or not, the phenomenon of the self-defense militia groups in western Michoacán is a clear sign of the lack of effective rule of law.

The Caballeros Templarios emerged from La Familia in 2011, and soon became a powerful cartel. Their semi-religious aspect and ideology was one of the factors in the cohesion of the group. The practice of these principles and the discipline the members followed seemed to have created a united force based on a brotherhood, and they appeared to have legitimized their cause and earned the respect of their communities. All of this started to crumble when the cartel's *modus operandi* shifted into a double-standards dogma. The group started to experience indiscipline and became as violent as the group they resented, the Zetas, losing legitimacy. The environment of violence and abuse the Caballeros Templarios created in their areas of influence incited a bottom-up participatory action from the civil society caught up in the conflict. In Michoacán, such participation took on more force when the self-defense groups established themselves as a dangerous enemy of the Templarios, having significant influence on the organization's weakening.

The cartel was set up with a pyramidal semi-religious structure. Highly centralized structures have proven to be more susceptible to strategies like the kingpin. Within the first three months of 2014, the Templarios lost three out its four main leaders. However, it was only after the capture of their last influential leader, La Tuta, in 2015 that the organization weakened significantly. The Templarios were not capable of restoring the organization after their top leaders were gone. Their survival capacity proved not to be strong enough.

The Templarios' presence and practice on Facebook presents similarities to the usage of the Sinaloa and the Zetas cartels. As in the other cases, their usage does not present statistical significance when it comes to attracting enemies and increasing targeting. Their utilization of YouTube, however, proved to have the opposite effect. La Tuta opted to use this platform to upload his own videos for different purposes. One purpose was to use it as a public relations outlet, trying to impose a benevolent vigilante image. YouTube was also the communication platform the cartel chose to send threatening messages to rival organizations, self-defense groups, and to Mexican security forces. This behavior differentiates La Tuta from other cartel leaders. In the Sinaloa case, high-ranking members and leaders of the organization such as El Chapo and his sons, or El Mayo, were also present on their social media platform, and, like La Tuta, they were highly active, but the platforms of choice and strategy differ. As argued in Chapter 2, leaders of the Sinaloa cartel on Twitter have presented a closed–open system. In other words, they maintain a wide base of fans and followers, but their exposure and interaction with them is mainly one-way. They have served as disseminators of information and rarely communicated directly with other followers. In their accounts, these leaders are followed by thousands, yet they only follow a close base of people. In addition, differently from La Tuta, the leaders of the Sinaloa cartel have been more careful about exposing their location and avoiding detection.

Finally, the Templarios' Facebook usage does not present indications of having had a negative effect or attracting attacks against the organization. For instance, *cybersicarios* celebrities such as El Broly fascinated many fans. But even though La Tuta tried to switch his strategy into a lower-profile mechanism, changing videos for audios, his exposure on YouTube presents positive statistical significance between an increase on his video appearances and the increase in the cartel's confrontations. In this case, social media worked as a double-edged sword. On the one hand, the platforms allowed them to get their benevolent message across with the purpose of gaining legitimacy, but, on the other, it made La Tuta more exposed which might have increased the chances of him being detected.

Notes

1 Some authors have pointed out that the organization had seven main leaders, adding Ignacio Rentería Andrade "El Nacho," or "El Cenizo," Samer José Servín Juárez, and Pablo Magaña "La Morsa" to the list (Reyez, 2014). Thus far, they have not been as influential as the other four leaders.
2 "*Cobro de piso*" or "*cobro por protección*" refers to a tax or fee cartels charge to business or street vendors to grant them permission to work and give them "protection." This is tactic similar to one that the Zetas and La Familia implemented.
3 Images originally retrieved from: https://worldwideweber2014.files.wordpress.com/2014/03/fbcartel-8-web.jpg and http://static.tvazteca.com/imagenes/2013/49/Presunto-sicario-presume-cuenta-Facebook-1874850.jpg (the latter was unavailable by the time of publication).
4 While conducting research, Twitter was not a feasible outlet in this case to develop a comprehensive analysis.
5 Video originally retrieved from: www.youtube.com/watch?v=i26jg4HvJJ8 (unavailable at the time of publication).
6 Video originally retrieved from: www.youtube.com/watch?v=4KdHgml4XiM (unavailable at the time of publication).
7 Video available at: www.youtube.com/watch?v=dgC0elu_UFU.
8 Available at: www.youtube.com/watch?v=ht1Y78sdsoQ.
9 Interview available at: www.youtube.com/watch?v=adz_lDG0fKw.
10 Footage originally retrieved from: www.youtube.com/watch?v=C1C-L2FBf0A (unavailable at the time of publication).
11 Footage available at: www.youtube.com/watch?v=7fLzgWvyYoQ.
12 Available at: www.youtube.com/watch?v=NtWQPV2R4jU.
13 Originally retrieved from: www.youtube.com/watch?v=KfE3pk2k-AI (unavailable at the time of publication).
14 Video available at: www.youtube.com/watch?v=kBDArEZwnK0.

References

Astorga, L. (2010). *Drug trafficking organizations and counter-drug strategies in the U.S.–Mexican context*. San Diego: Center for U.S.–Mexican Studies. University of California in San Diego.
BBC Mundo (2012). Encuentran 13 cadáveres en Michoacán. BBC News. Retrieved from:www.bbc.com/mundo/ultimas_noticias/2012/01/120109_ultnot_michoacan_muertos_jgc.
Bunker, R. J., & Keshavarz, A. (Eds.). (2019). *Los Caballeros Templarios de Michoacán: Imagery, symbolism, and narratives*. Small Wars Journal-El Centro eBook.
Bunker, R. J., & Sullivan, J. P. (2019). "Holy Warriors" Excerpt. In R. J. Bunker & A. Keshavarz (Eds.), *Los Caballeros Templarios de Michoacán: Imagery, symbolism, and narratives*. Small Wars Journal-El Centro eBook.
Castellanos J. F. (2016). "Michoacán vive una calma frágil", dice Aureoles en su primer informe. *Proceso*. Retrieved from: https://justiceinmexico.org/organized-crime-related-incidents-occur-michoacan/.
Congressional Research Service. (2019). *Mexico: Organized crime and drug trafficking organizations*. CRS Report. Retrieved from: https://fas.org/sgp/crs/row/R41576.pdf.

Cox, J. (2013). Mexico's drug cartels love social media. *Borderland Beat*. Retrieved from: www.borderlandbeat.com/2013/11/mexicos-drug-cartels-love-social-media.html.

Excélsior (2014). Nazario Moreno González, "El Chayo." Retrieved from: www.excelsior.com.mx/topico/nazario-moreno-gonzalez-el-chayo.

Garay Salamanca, L. J., & Salcedo-Albarán, E. (2011). *Drug trafficking corruption and states: How illicit networks reconfigure institutions in Colombia, Guatemala and Mexico*. Bogotá, Colombia: Fundación Método.

Grillo, I. (2006). Mexico cracks down on violence. *Seattle Post-Intelligencer*. Associated Press. Retrieved from: www.seattlepi.com/national/295578_mexico12.html.

Grillo, I. (2014, May 20). Autodefensas, heroes o villanos? *Letras Libres*. Retrieved from: www.letraslibres.com/mexico-espana/autodefensas-heroes-o-villanos.

Guardian (2014). Mexican vigilante leader Hipólito Mora arrested over the murders of two men. Retrieved from: www.theguardian.com/world/2014/mar/12/mexico-vigilante-leader-hipolita-mora-arrested-murders-two-men-drugs-cartel.

Infobae (2019, August 21). Radriografía de la narcoguerra en Michoacán: quienes y por que regreso la violencia al estado. Retrieved from: www.infobae.com/america/mexico/2019/08/21/radiografia-de-la-narcoguerra-en-michoacan-quienes-y-por-que-regreso-la-violencia-al-estado/.

InSight Crime. (2017a). Knights Templar. Retrieved from: www.insightcrime.org/mexico-organized-crime-news/knights-templar-profile/.

InSight Crime. (2017b). Servando Gomez Martinez, alias, "La Tuta." Retrieved from: www.insightcrime.org/mexico-organized-crime-news/servando-gomez-martinez-la-tuta/.

Kail, T. M. (2019). Battle of the Brotherhood: The war between the Caballeros Templarios and the Freemasons of Michoacán. In R. J. Bunker & A. Keshavarz (Eds.), *Los Caballeros Templarios de Michoacán: Imagery, symbolism, and narratives*. Small Wars Journal-El Centro eBook.

Keene, R. (2019). Mexico's Knight Templar and Code of Conduct implications. In R. J. Bunker & A. Keshavarz (Eds.), *Los Caballeros Templarios de Michoacán: Imagery, symbolism, and narratives* (pp. 65–77). Small Wars Journal- El Centro Book.

Lomnitz, C. (2019). The ethos and telos of Michoacán's Knights Templar. *Representations*, 147(1), 96–123.

Lucio, R. (2015). Where in the world is Broly Banderas? *Borderland Beat*. Retrieved from: www.borderlandbeat.com/2015/03/what-happened-to-broly-banderas.html.

Marquez, J. (2006). Decapitan a 5 en Uruapan; tiran cabezas en un bar. *El Universal*. Retrieved from: https://archivo.eluniversal.com.mx/estados/62434.html.

Morales, A., & Rivera Ramirez, L. (2011, June 22). Cae jefe de cartel de "La Familia." *El Universal*.

Najar, A. (2014, April 21). Los crueles rituals de iniciacion del narco en Mexico. BBC Mundo. Retrieved from: www.bbc.com/mundo/noticias/2014/04/140410_mexico_rituales_narcotrafico_templarios_an.

Otero, S. (2011). "Templarios," prioridad militar. *El Universal*. Retrieved from: https://archivo.eluniversal.com.mx/nacion/186558.html.

Pineda, L. (2013, May 22). El Gobierno envía 5,000 soldados y policías a Michoacán para combatir el narco. *El Faro*. Retrieved from: www.elfaro.net/es/201305/internacionales/12150/El-Gobierno-env%C3%ADa-5000-soldados-y-polic%C3%ADas-a-Michoac%C3%A1n-para-combatir-el-narco.htm?st-full_text=all&tpl=11.

Reyez, J. (2014). Caballeros Templarios, entrenados por Estados Unidos, Egipto e Israel. Red Voltaire. Retrieved from: www.voltairenet.org/article185487.html.

Conclusion

There is a dialectical interplay between the positive and the dark sides with regard to the rise of the usage of social media (Arquilla & Ronfeldt, 2001). On the one hand, the opportunities these new communication channels offer – such as serving as organizing mechanisms, the hope of moving towards more transparent democracies, the rise of a stronger civil society – stimulated the hopes of scholars and activists for greater civic participation, governance, and governmental accountability. These hopes developed principally after several powerful mass demonstrations around the world arose such as the Arab Spring, and protests in Tunisia and Moldova (Morozov, 2009). Empirical evidence suggests that the so-called "Twitter revolutions" have been successful at overturning long-standing authoritarian establishments, for example, the Mubarak regime in Egypt. In Mexico, some social movements started as a response to the high rates of violence caused by the drug war. One of them was called *Movimiento por la Paz*, led by poet Javier Sicilia whose son was assassinated by members of a drug cartel. Another example has civilians organizing and protesting during the anniversary of the disappearance of the 43 students from Ayotzinapa, Guerrero. Unfortunately, none of these social actions carried through with much force: some Arab countries have failed to reestablish politically, and in Mexico the drug war is bloodier than ever. On the other hand, the dual nature of social media platforms presents a darker side dominated mainly by criminal organizations and terrorist groups.

This book focuses on the dark side of social media and systematically analyzes its usage by three criminal organizations: the Sinaloa cartel, the Zetas, and the Caballeros Templarios. The amount of information members of the cartels provide on these communication outlets is vast, impressively detailed, at times sweet and humane, at other times violent and horrific. Reviewing the content of their profiles and YouTube videos spurs a rollercoaster of emotions. The visuals range from love letters to decapitated bodies.

Through this study, I found that the strategic adaptation of social media platforms has different effects on criminal organization's survival capacity. The empirical evidence suggests that if used efficiently, social media is a tool that provides benefits and strengthens drug cartels in Mexico, enhancing both their organizational and their operational capabilities. What follows is an overview of the empirical findings and the conceptual contributions and theoretical outcomes. Finally, this book closes by proposing some policy recommendations and prospects for a future research agenda.

Levels of Survival Capacity

I evaluate the cartels' capacity to survive in two stages. The first chronicles the context under which these organizations fight and their capacity to respond to major organizational shocks. The second surveys the cartels' social media presence and usage.

In the first phase, the data gathered gives an indication of the operational environment of each particular drug cartel studied here, including: the geographical importance of their territories, the extent of their domains, and the organization's frequency of attacks and main enemies. Three main findings are derived from the analysis: (i) drug cartels' levels of survival capacity; (ii) the symmetrical and asymmetrical relations between actors in terms of capabilities; and (iii) a fluctuation in the targeting of criminal organizations by the Mexican security forces.

By monitoring fluctuations in the cartels' rate of violence and criminal activities before and after organizational setbacks, it was possible to establish different levels of survival capacity. The Sinaloa cartel was the case that presented the highest level of survival capacity. In comparison with the Zetas and the Caballeros Templarios, after a restructuring process, the cartel's response to organizational setbacks, especially after El Chapo's capture, showed minor destabilization, but relative solidity in their violence and the continuation of their criminal activities. The Zetas presented a medium level of survival capacity, their transition from a military-hierarchical towards a highly decentralized structure allowing the organization to readapt better after major organizational disruptions. However, the cartel's internal fracturing has led to its debilitation and fragmentation. The Zetas have recently divided into two organizations; an older generation of drug traffickers have stayed as the Zetas Vieja Escuela (Zetas Old School), with the other group being the Cartel del Noreste (CDN). This last group is currently fighting for turf and key trafficking ports in northern Tamaulipas, Nuevo León and Coahuila, areas that are experiencing an upsurge of violence. The aggressive and expansionist strategy the CDN is implementing was one the Zetas used during their early days. Although CDN is becoming a powerful and aggressive cartel, the Zetas Vieja Escuela remains relevant to the drug trafficking scene. The Caballeros Templarios presented a low level of survival capacity. This cartel, after the capture of its four main leaders, was not able to restructure as a cohesive group, leaving just scattered cells operating and the organization weakened considerably.

132 Conclusion

The data gathered on the cartels' confrontations facilitated a comparison of each organization with its main rivals in terms of capabilities. For instance, the Sinaloa cartel is the organization that was the most targeted by the Mexican authorities between 2013 and 2015. In addition, it is the cartel that has been targeted the most by foreign governments, including the U.S. and countries in Europe. The survival of the Sinaloa organization in the face of such intense national and international law enforcement pressure indicates a high degree of strength. The Zetas displayed greater vulnerability when they surrendered to non-state actors' threats as exemplified by what happened during the altercation with the activist group Anonymous. In the case of the Caballeros Templarios, self-defense militia groups, some of them backed by the Peña Nieto's government, left it unable to adapt and survive the attacks of other non-state actors. These examples shed light on the different capabilities of each of these criminal organizations. Finally, the figures demonstrate that the frequency and rate of intensity at which security forces targeted the cartels from 2006 to 2015 have fluctuated. For example, significant decreases in clashes between various security forces and a specific drug cartel can be an indicator of collusion and corruption from part of the authorities.

The second part of this study explored the Mexican drug cartels' presence on and usage of social media and the effects on their survival capacity. The findings suggest that the cartels' usage of these communication channels varied in the selection of platforms and strategies, which in turn, led to different outcomes for their effectiveness of execution. The implementation of social network analysis in this study proved to be a useful tool to better understand and study criminal organizations. Furthermore, the analysis provided important information about the central figures, reach of the networks, interests, subnetworks, rivals, and demographics, and produced a visual representation for each cartel's network on social media. The following cartel characteristics were revealed: (i) the organizations' "social capital"; (ii) their online organizational model; and (iii) behavioral patterns.

By conducting a social network analysis, it was possible to uncover the cartels' social capital on social media. Put differently, the interpersonal or relational properties between agents or nodes, the varied nature of relationships, and the way the information flows through the organizations' networks were brought into focus. For example, the graph of the Sinaloa cartel suggests that the most central agent in the network is El Chapo. El Chapo's Twitter account registered a high outward degree of centrality, meaning that he serves as a major disseminator of information, followed by the accounts of his sons Alfredo and Ivan Archivaldo Guzmán. In the Zetas' network, centrality is not so much concentrated in one individual since several agents share high degrees of centrality, the main capos of this organization not being visible on their Facebook network. Their network also shows a node with a high degree of betweenness, meaning that this particular member of the Zetas serves as the structural bridge than holds the network together; taking away this node from their network would have major repercussions. In the Caballeros Templarios network, the information flows are reciprocal since their nodes exchange information with one another more than in the other two cases.

Each cartel presented different types of online organizational models and in two cases, the Sinaloa cartel and the Zetas, their virtual structural model was reminiscent of their physical configuration. In other words, their physical organization and networks translate into the virtual world, also unveiling the groups or clusters into which the organization divides. The Twitter social network graph of the Sinaloa cartel reflects a hub-and-spokes structure, and it is composed of different clusters. For example, different groups that worked under El Chapo's faction, such as *Los Antrax*, *la Gente Nueva*, or *los Damaso*, are visible in their network. The Zetas' Facebook network shows a decentralized structure and the formation of new subnetworks or groups is depicted. During the timeframe of this study, the emergence of Cartel del Noreste from the Zetas' network was identifiable. I was able to detect the early formation of a criminal cell that later became its own cartel and a principal enemy of the Zetas. The Facebook network graph of the Caballeros Templarios cartel did not replicate their physical structure, but it did reflect the transition of some members from La Familia Michoacana to the Templarios. It also hinted at their former connection with the Zetas.

Johnson et al. (2016) proposed that by examining the online behavior of criminal organizations, behavioral patterns can be identified, making possible the prediction of future conduct. For example, through the Twitter and Facebook network graphs, especially those of the Sinaloa and the Zetas cartels, the formation of subgroups was traced and monitored. Early detection of these cells reveals indications of initial signals of fragmentation or the emergence of new cartels. A good example of this is the split of the Zetas from the Gulf cartel, and later the split of the CDN from the Zetas.

Additionally, throughout the content analysis of the accounts of members of the Mexican drug cartels, I found that, besides showing off their fancy cars and luxurious life, the cartels follow specific social media strategies, some more benevolent than others. The Sinaloa cartel and the Caballeros Templarios followed a similar strategy, one focused on emphasizing social acceptance. The purpose of this approach is to gain legitimacy in the communities the groups operate in, in order for them to conduct their business more effectively. The tactic also served as a force multiplier, promoting a lifestyle that attracted new recruits. In both cases, leaders of the cartels were highly visible on social media. El Chapo, for years, had an active Twitter account followed by thousands of fans, including celebrities and politicians, and Servando Gómez "La Tuta" for a couple of years uploaded videos on YouTube. Although their tactics followed a similar path, there is a key difference between the two. On the one hand, El Chapo used Twitter as an open–closed system of communication, meaning that while a couple of hundred thousand followed him, he only interacted with just a few accounts. On the other hand, La Tuta used YouTube in order to upload videos of him explaining the origins and vigilante mission of the Caballeros Templarios. Due to the double discourse his organization followed, he was not as successful at gaining legitimacy from the citizenry as El Chapo. The data presented in this case suggests that the videos he uploaded to YouTube gave information about his surroundings, making him an easier target for the authorities and self-defense militia groups. The Zetas used a different strategy that consisted mostly of conducting psychological warfare. They effectively utilized social media platforms as an extension for inciting terror in the municipalities they operate in. contrast to the Sinaloa cartel, the Zetas conducted their business not through social legitimacy but though coercion and intimidation.

When assessing the relationship between the drug cartels' usage of social media and cartels' confrontations, the Sinaloa cartel's exposure on social media did not increase targeting from their rivals. Similarly, the Zetas presented a negative and statistically significant relationship between the two variables but the relationship is weak. The same results applied to the Caballeros Templarios and their Facebook usage. La Tuta's exposure on YouTube, however, increased the visibility and targeting of the Templarios' leader, displaying a strong statistical correlation.

Comparing the three cases, six major points are drawn from the analysis. Table 6.1 presents a summary of the empirical findings:

i. Criminal organizations operating under structures with some level of decentralization, such as hub-and-spokes, coupled with a *modus operandi* on the more traditional side of the spectrum, present a high level of resistance. This is the case with the Sinaloa cartel.
ii. Criminal organizations with a more decentralized type of structure, such as franchises, and working under a non-traditional *modus operandi* present a medium level of survival capacity like the Zetas.
iii. Criminal organizations with highly centralized or hierarchical structures, operating under a non-traditional *modus operandi* demonstrate a low level of survival capacity. This is the case with the Caballeros Templarios.
iv. The most successful social media strategy that cartels have followed is to use these communication platforms as a tool to construct relatability from the citizenship towards the drug cartel, emphasizing social acceptance and using the platform as a force multiplier. Coupled with an open–closed communications tactic, this can strengthen a criminal organization.
v. Following a psychological warfare strategy shows effective results, up to a point. The criminal organization can have control of its territories through coercion, but might gain resentment from society which in the end works against them.
vi. Overexposure on social media, especially on platforms with high levels of visual information, increases the possibility of attacks from rivals.

Table 6.1 Summary of Empirical Findings

Case	Structure	Modus Operandi	Social Media Presence	Main platforms of Preference	Strategies	Effectiveness of Social Media Strategy	Social Media Usage and Reported Clashes Statistical Correlation	Level of Survival Capacity
Sinaloa cartel	Hub-and-spokes	Traditional	High	Twitter	• Inform the public about their operations and missions • Promote lifestyle • Emphasize social acceptance • Force multiplier • Send threatening messages • Top leaders exposed but maintaining a degree of discretion • Most central nodes serve as disseminators of information	Effective	Negative and not significant	High
The Zetas	From military-hierarchical to franchise	Non-traditional	Medium	Facebook	• Psychological warfare • Incite terror • Send threatening messages • Promote the organization through *narcoraps* • Top leadership maintains a low profile on social media	Effective	Negative significant but weak	Medium
Caballeros Templarios	Semi-religious hierarchical	Non-traditional	Medium	YouTube	• Emphasize social acceptance • Top leadership overexposed in YouTube videos	Not as effective	Statistically significant and somewhat strong	Low

Conceptual Contributions

Some scholars (i.e., Williams & Godson, 2002; Arquilla & Ronfeldt, 2001) have suggested that there is a need to broaden the conceptualization of criminal organizations. As this study has demonstrated, criminal organizations that present a higher degree of survival capacity are the ones that have adopted a more decentralized, networked kind of structure. The current definition of drug cartels or criminal organizations is deficient or inadequate when it comes to describing the new generation of contemporary forms of organized crime. Moreover, since most of these groups have also diversified their illicit activities, the conceptualization of organized crime must change to consider the new variants. This book joins a growing body of scholarship that argues that the new generation of criminal organizations should be denoted instead as *criminal networks*.

The cases compared in this study present different structural configurations. For example, the Sinaloa cartel works under a hub-and-spokes structure that has a degree of decentralization. The Zetas cartel shifted from a military-hierarchical to a highly decentralized franchise structure, both displaying a degree of compartmentalization. In contrast, the Caballeros Templarios maintained a semi-religious hierarchical alignment which proved to be less adequate in the contemporary arena of drug trafficking. In sum, the cases with greater decentralization and flatter structures proved to be more resistant to organizational disruptions.

As theory states, structural flatness intensifies the survival capacity of criminal organizations in several ways: (i) it decreases response time, (ii) it decentralizes decision-making, allowing for faster restructuring and greater adaptability, and (iii) increases flexibility, minimizing the impacts when leadership is removed, since these central actors have been insulated.

The literature suggests that the use of social media has worked as a tool that facilitates and enhances the functionality of decentralized structures. In the case of the Sinaloa cartel, the integration of social media into their strategies gave beneficial results. These platforms have contributed to their strengthening in a number of ways, such as increasing the flow of information that allows a decentralized structure to function. This can be reflected in the real-time messaging that is possible through these web-based outlets. As Arquilla and Ronfeldt (2001) put it, "new information technologies render the ability to connect and coordinate the actions of widely distributed nodes ... whoever masters this form will accrue advantages at a substantial nature" (p. 5). Another favorable feature of social media is that it aids in establishing direct channels of communication to promote social acceptability. Studies suggest that the social and cultural embedding of a cartel in the areas where they operate is indispensable for these groups to successfully conduct their illicit business. The Sinaloa cartel has adequately used these platforms to their advantage. Stern and Berger (2015) recognize that social media has opened the door to alternative types of interaction that have reinforced connectivity, contributing to the strengthening of criminal organizations. The Sinaloa cartel social media strategy emphasizes social mechanisms, building trust and legitimacy between their organization and society, and this has helped them to create a *clientelistic* relationship. As social acceptability of the cartel grows, so does their ability to recruit people and to naturalize the narco culture. Finally, they have used these platforms as a force multiplier. Besides being protected by a social net, some cartels have been able to attract a greater workforce, which is imperative for their survival capacity, since they quickly find replacements for soldiers captured or lost in battles.

As mentioned above, this study finds that the Zetas' usage of social media differs from the Sinaloa cartel's strategy. This criminal organization, better known for their hyper-violent *modus operandi*, found in social media a medium through which they could extend this strategy. The social media content of this group presents the most vile and grotesque pictures and footage. Their main online strategy is to use these outlets as tool for psychological warfare. Their online presence is similar to their physical presence in the sense that in both planes their main business model is to intimidate their enemies and instigate fear in the population. Scholars such as Farwell (2014) and Dale (2014) argue that this approach can be effective for the organization to maintain control through fear in their domains, but also can work to their disadvantage since they can be prompting the resentment of society. This has been called the "social media paradox."

The Caballeros Templarios show a better example of the social media paradox. This is the only case that showed that the adoption of social media had negative repercussions on their survival capacity. The overexposure of their main leader La Tuta on YouTube indicates that it might have contributed to his location by the authorities. Although members of this cartel also have a presence on Facebook, their activity on this platform does not show any suggestion that it attracted more targeting by rival groups and security forces. Their use of social media has been inconsistent. One of the main purposes of their social media strategy is to portray the organization as a benevolent one, serving as protector of its communities. They also show deep religious roots. In the physical world, however, they behave differently. As in the case of the Zetas, the Caballeros Templarios also gained the resentment of society, who responded with the creation of strong self-defense groups in western Michoacán.

Policy Recommendations

Based on this study, I propose three main possible policy recommendations. Some focus on short-term opportunities that the monitoring of the cartels' activity on social media provide in shaping government strategies to fight these criminal organizations. Others are long-term and consist of cooperation efforts between the intelligence community and security forces.

A first recommendation is to rethink the concept utilized to understand the new networked, decentralized nature of strong criminal organizations. This will help policy makers to recognize the challenges of dealing with these type of groups and reformulate targeting strategies. The second is the consolidation of information systems and collaboration among the different intelligence bodies in Mexico in cooperation with the intelligence communities of other countries. This will allow the monitoring and processing of real-time information that members of the cartels provide through social media. Last is the implementation of social network analysis into the strategies to fight organized crime. As my research shows, structural holes and network vulnerabilities can be detected. In addition, changes in the cartels' networks can be monitored as in, for example, the early detection of subgroups forming that might later become an independent and powerful criminal group.

Current State of Affairs

The landscape and context under which the drug trafficking industry operates in Mexico is constantly changing. As the drug war continues, criminal organizations and their business models adapt and react to the strategies and drug policies implemented by governments. In Mexico, the metastasis of cartels continues and violence is escalating, every year superseding the previous one for the number of drug-related homicides. In 2018, there were 33,341 homicides (SESNSP, 2018), and it is projected that 2019 will close with 36,000 (*Expansión*, 2019).

On December 1, 2018 the administration of Andrés Manuel López Obrador (ALMO) and his leftist political party MORENA (*Movimiento de Regeneración Nacional*) took office, after an overwhelming victory over the mainstream political parties in Mexico. AMLO inherited a violent country, and the drug trafficking panorama during his first year in office is reaching yet another level. The security strategy put forward by the Mexican president has concentrated in two areas. First, he has started to target the *huachicoleros* (oil thieves). He mandated the closing of dozens of pipes through which members of cartels stole the product to sell it on the black market. This tactic produced an upsurge of violence in some central states such as Guanajuato and Puebla. The second approach is the creation of a new security body called the National Guard to replace the military in their role of combating the cartels. As of now, both are fighting criminal organizations. AMLO's discourse surrounding the war is different from previous administrations. His party is developing an *Amnesty Law*, which will absolve small-scale drug traffickers of their crimes. He has also mentioned the possibility of moving forward with providing amnesty to high-profile drug traffickers in order to achieve peace. The president has stated that he wants to pursue a strategy of *"abrazos no balazos"* (hugs instead of guns/shootings).

His evasiveness, in a sense, has worsened the conditions of the conflict in Mexico. As mentioned in earlier chapters, newer cartels are rising, stronger and with a business model even more violent that the Zetas, such as the Cartel Jalisco Nueva Generación, Cartel del Noreste, Los Viagras, or Cartel de Santa Rosa de Lima.

Two recent events seem to have set a new era for the drug trafficking arena in Mexico. One was the failed detention of El Chapo's son Ovidio Guzmán in Culiacán, Sinaloa in October, 2019. As the Mexican military captured Guzmán, allies and members of the Sinaloa cartel rapidly organized in an ambush to pressure the government to free Ovidio. After a series of phone calls, the liberation of some prisoners by members of the cartel, and the threat to start shootings creating chaos across Culiacán, targeting innocent people, the government decided to let him go. This choice has brought to light many questions, such as: Are Mexican cartels more powerful than the state? The following month, in November, nine members of the LeBaron family were assassinated by a criminal organization in the state of Coahuila. The act is particularly atrocious because it included the murder of six young children. These two cases indicate that the new wave of criminal organizations in Mexico are becoming more ruthless than ever. They do not care about killing innocent civilians, not even children, in order to get their messages across and to conduct their business. These groups are showing yet another level of inhumanity never experienced before.

The use of social media remains a common practice for cartels in Mexico. Their virtual *modus operandi* is also evolving. For example, they have expanded their extortion methods and are using Facebook messenger or WhatsApp to conduct this illegal activity. New criminal organizations are adopting social media strategies, following the model of other organizations and taking it further.

Future Research Agenda

This study focuses on the usage of social media by criminal organizations. This research presents challenges since it is one of the first research works that attempts to analyze usage and impacts systematically. With this said, there is room for improvement. The social network analysis presented for each case can be studied further, amplifying the network representation. In addition, it can be applied to younger but powerful criminal organizations such as Cartel Jalisco Nueva Generación and Cartel del Noreste, extending the temporal bracket of this study.

The research design applied for this analysis can be extrapolated to the study of criminal organizations in other countries such as criminal bands in Brazil, which seem to be following a similar pattern of adopting social media into their operational tactics. Criminal organizations such as Primeiro Comando da Capital (PCC), Comando Vermelho (CV), and Terceiro

Comando Puro (TPC) in Brazil, and some of their capos, such as Nando Bacalhau (arrested in 2012) and Marcelo Santos das Dores, have a presence on social media outlets. Another example is the powerful gangs based mainly in Central America, such as Barrio 18 and the MS-13, which are not only using social media for propaganda purposes, but are taking advantage of the information people post on their accounts to monitor possible victims for kidnapping and extortion.

In the research presented in this book, it is evident that the information revolution is altering the nature of conflict. The self-censorship of traditional media outlets together with the adoption of social media as a main source of information about the drug war transformed the latter's dynamics, so that it has transitioned into a multilayered conflict. This investigation can be taken into a broader study of conflicts in the international relations field.

The drug conflict in Mexico is far from being over: violence is increasing every year, drugs keep crossing borders, and consumption is growing around the world. More countries are starting to depart from the punitive model and adopting alternative drug policies. Amongst these cases are Portugal and Uruguay, which are approaching the drug problem through different policies, decriminalization and legalization, respectively. Both have shown some promising results. As the drug industry morphs, drug policies should adapt as well. A change in strategy and drug policy in Mexico is imperative.

References

Arquilla, J., & Ronfeldt, D. (2001). *Networks and netwars*. RAND.
Dale, H. (2014). Social media prove double-edged sword for ISIS. *The Daily Signal*. Available at: www.dailysignal.com/2014/10/23/social-media-prove-double-edged-sword-isis/.
Expansión (2019, December 3). 2019 cerrara con 36,000 homicidios y solo 1 de cada 10 se castiga: reports. *Expansión Política*. Retrieved from: https://politica.expansion.mx/mexico/2019/12/03/2019-cerrara-con-36-000-homicidios-y-solo-1-de-cada-10-se-castiga-reportes.
Farwell, J. P. (2014). The media strategy of ISIS. *Global Politics and Strategy*, 56(6), 49–55.
Johnson, N. F., Zhen, M., Vorobyeva, Y., Gabrield, A., Qi, H., Velasquez, N., Manrique, P., Johnson, D., Restrepo, E., Song, C., & Wuchty, S. (2016, June 17). New online ecology of adversarial aggregates: ISIS and beyond. Science, 352(6292), 1459–1463.
Morozov, E. (2009). Moldova's Twitter revolution. *Foreign Policy*. Retrieved from: http://neteffect.foreingpolicy.com/posts/2009/04/07/moldovas_twitter_revolution.
SESNSP. (2018). *Secreatariado Ejecutive del Sistema Nacional de Seguridad Publica*. Retrieved from: www.gob.mx/sesnsp.
Stern, J., & Berger, J. M. (2015). *ISIS: The state of terror*. London: William Collins.
Williams, P., & Godson, R. (2002). Anticipating organized and transnational crime. *Crime, Law and Social Change*, 37(4), 311–355.

Appendix

Appendix A. Social Media Utilization Indicators

Facebook	• Yes/no • Number of accounts • Number of friends	• Year of opening/closing the account • Frequency of posts • Date of last post • Active/not active • Private/public	• Recruiting • PR • Psychological warfare • Recruitment	• Positive/negative comments from friends
Twitter	• Yes/no • Reach (numbers of followers)		• Propaganda • PR • Psychological warfare • Recruitment	• Positive/negative comments from followers
YouTube	• Yes/no • Number of videos		• Propaganda • PR • Psychological warfare • Recruitment	• Positive/negative comments from viewers

Index

Al Qaeda 20, 36–7, 40–1, 65
AMLO *see* Lopez Obrador, A.M
amnesty 138
Ayotzinapa 20, 132

BACRIM *see* criminal bands
ballon effect 20, 24
Barrio 18, 20, 140
Beltrán Leyva (BLO) 4, 53, 67, 75, 78
betweenness 7, 61, 71, 88, 115, 132
BLO *see* Beltrán Leyva
Blog del narco 47, 67, 92, 94, 118
Bolivia 19, 24, 88
Brazil 12, 20, 139–40
Bush, G.W. 19, 20

Cali cartel 16, 76
Cárdenas Guillén, O. 76-7, 83
Caro Quintero, R. 53, 68
Cartel del Noreste (CDN) 2, 10, 78, 85, 88, 96, 131, 133
Cartel Jalisco New Generation (CJNG) 2, 21, 54, 78, 108, 110, 116, 120, 140
Carteles Unidos (CU) 78, 95
cash cows 25
CDN *see* Cartel del Noreste
central nodes 7, 10, 12, 37, 61, 63, 72, 88, 111, 114–15
centrality 7, 61, 63, 71, 87–8, 115, 132
CJNG *see* Cartel Jalisco New Generation
Clinton, H. 61
cobro de piso 107, 119
cocaine 16, 24, 57–9, 75–7, 105
cockroach effect 20, 24
collateral damage 15, 24, 31

Colombia 12, 16–17, 19, 20, 24, 56, 58, 60–1
Comando Vermelho (CV) 139
corruption 4, 16, 18–19, 25–6, 39, 106, 132
COs *see* criminal networks
criminal bands 139
criminal networks 12, 29, 39, 78
CU *see* Carteles Unidos
CV *see* Comando Vermelho
cybersicario 105, 113, 126
cyberwar 43

DEA *see* Drug Enforcement Administration
decentralization 10, 25–6, 85, 88, 134, 136
Democratic Revolutionary Party (PRD) 18
democratization 27
direct centrality 7
double-funnel model 24
Drug Enforcement Administration (DEA) 21
drug kingpin statute 77
drug trafficking organizations (DTOs) 10, 16, 18, 26, 52, 70
DTOs *see* Drug Trafficking Organizations

Ecuador 56, 60
edges 7, 61, 87, 114–15
Egypt 36–8, 130
Ejécito Zapatista de Liberación Nacional (EZLN) 17
El Milenio 106
El Universal 55
elite-exploitative model 25

EZLN *see* Ejército Zapatista de Liberación Nacional

FBI *see* Federal Bureau of Investigation
Federal Bureau of Investigation (FBI) 77
Felix Gallardo, M.A. 17, 53
Fox, V. 17, 55
franchise 77, 99, 134, 136

GAFES *see* Mexican Army's Airborne Special Group Forces
globalization 23
Gomez, S. 11, 105–7, 112–13, 122, 133
Google 43, 52, 98
Grupo de Armas y Tácticas Especiales (GATES) 80
Guadalajara cartel 53
guerrilla groups 41
Gulf cartel 10, 42–3, 46, 57, 75–7, 79, 80–4, 88, 99, 104, 106, 133
Guzman, A. 10, 54, 61, 63, 65, 71, 132
Guzman, I.A. 10, 54, 63, 65, 71, 132
Guzman, Joaquin "El Chapo" 10, 21, 52–5, 57–8, 60–1, 63, 65–8, 70–1, 126, 131–4, 139
Guzman Lopez, O. 55, 61, 139

Honduras 56, 80
hub-and-spokes 53, 61, 72, 133–4, 136
human rights violations 15, 22, 25

illicit networks 39
INEGI *see* National Institute of Statistics and Geography
institutional weakness 4
International Criminal Police Organization (INTERPOL) 58
ISIS 9, 36–8, 41–2, 63, 65

Justice Attorney's Office (PGR) 6, 60, 76, 111

Kaibilies 75
kingpin strategy 72

La Familia Michoacana 44, 79, 106, 115, 133
Lazcano Lazcano, H. 67, 77–8, 82–5, 88, 100
Lopez Obrador, A.M. 1, 11, 18, 138

Los Viagras 108, 139
Lupsha, P.A. 25

maquiladoras 17
Mara Salvatrucha (MS-13) 20, 75, 140
marijuana 16, 53, 77, 105
Marines Secretariat (SEMAR) 65
Medellin cartel 16, 19
media censorship 44, 69, 95
media curator 43
Merida Initiative 18–20
Merkel, Angela 52
Mexican Army's Airborne Special Group Forces (GAFES) 76
Mexico City 56–7, 67
militarization 2, 15, 22, 24, 31, 44, 108
militarization trap 31
military-hierarchical structure 77, 85, 99, 131, 136
Mireles, J.M. 108, 110
Moldova 36, 130
Morales Treviño, M.A. 77–8, 83, 85
Morales Treviño, O. 77–8, 81, 83, 89, 96
MORENA *see* National Revolutionary Movement
Moreno, N. 104, 106–7, 111, 116–17, 119, 122
Movimiento por la paz 130
MS-13 *see* Mara Salvatrucha
Mubarak 36, 130

NAFTA *see* North American Free Trade Agreement
narcoculture 67, 72, 91
narconews 67, 118
narcorridos 28, 45, 67, 90, 118
National Action Party (PAN) 17, 30, 55
National Institute of Statistics and Geography (INEGI) 6
National Revolutionary Movement (MORENA) 138
neoliberal regimes 4, 23
Netflix 28, 52
Netherlands 56, 104
Nicaragua 56
Nixon, R. 20, 24
NodeXL 6, 86
non-traditional cartels 55, 78, 110
North American Free Trade Agreement (NAFTA) 17, 23

Operación Michoacán 108

PAN *see* National Action Party
Panama 56
paramilitary 17, 108
Peña Nieto, E. 1, 9, 15, 20–1, 54, 61, 65, 68, 83, 108, 132
Peru 19, 24, 60, 88
PGR *see* Justice Attorney's Office
Pimentel, S.A. 25
Plan Colombia 19
plaza 58, 77, 82–3, 104, 107–8, 119
Portugal 140
poverty theory 28
PRD *see* Democratic Revolutionary Party
PRI *see* Revolutionary Institutional Party
Primeiro Comando da Capital (PCC) 139
psychological warfare 10, 38, 96, 100, 134, 137

rational choice 28
resilience 8, 39
Revolutionary Institutional Party (PRI) 16–18, 20, 25–7, 30

Santa Rosa de Lima cartel 139
Secretary of National Defense (SEDENA) 65, 88, 108
securitization 15, 18
SEDENA *see* Secretary of National Defense
self-defense groups 43, 79, 108–10, 113–14, 116, 118–19, 125–6, 132, 134, 137

SEMAR *see* Marines Secretariat
six degrees of separation 39
SNA *see* social network analysis
social media paradox 11, 37, 42, 137
sovereignty 22
SSM *see* Standard Security Model
Standard Security Model (SSM) 19
syncretism 91

Tamaulipas 42, 46, 76–7, 79–80, 86, 93, 98, 100, 111
Terceiro Comando Puro (TCP) 139
The New York Times 85
tierra caliente 105, 108, 119
Tijuana cartel 75, 106
traditional cartels 75, 78
Trump, D. 61, 65
Tunisia 36, 130
Twitter revolutions 36, 130

Uruguay 60, 140

Vietnam War 16

Washington 19
watchdog 44
World War II (WWII) 46

Zamabada, I. 54–5, 57–8, 61, 63, 67–9, 95, 126
Zetas Old School 2, 11, 78, 88, 131

Printed in the United States
by Baker & Taylor Publisher Services